THE UNOFFICIAL

BEETLEJUICE! BEETLEJUICE! BEETLEJUICE! COOKBOOK

75+ darkly delicious recipes inspired by the Tim Burton classic

Hugo Award Winner

Thea James

Recipes by Isabel Minunni

INTRODUCTION

As a kid, I was always a little different. Strange. Unusual, even. My family moved around a lot thanks to my father's job, meaning that I was always the "new girl"—the novelty kid, trying to fit in, eager to be seen but also happy to fly under the radar. When you're always new, you find solitary ways to amuse yourself. For me, that meant a whole lot of books and movies. One of those movies (as you might have guessed since you're reading this introduction) was Tim Burton's early masterpiece, *Beetlejuice*.

A reverse-haunted house story in which the ghosts are being terrorized by the living, *Beetlejuice* was flat-out hilarious to me. This was my first introduction to Michael Keaton, and Beetlejuice*—not his incredibly cool Batman or even the guy who photocopies himself in *Multiplicity*—will forever be the default role I associate with him. But really, a large part of the reason *Beetlejuice* became so special to me personally is Winona Ryder's Lydia Deetz. Another (smartass) kid who got moved around by her parents, eager to be seen and heard, unapologetically skeptical of everything yet willing to believe in ghosts, Lydia was a girl after my own heart. I admired and identified with her flair for the melodramatic and, despite her overt edge, her desire to do right by her parents and the Maitlands. Also, she had a killer wardrobe, a super cool camera collection and sweet dance moves.

Lydia made me realize that being strange and unusual was a good thing. And now, thanks to the *Beetlejuice*-inspired recipes in this book, all of us strange and unusual types can gather with each other, our families and maybe even our friends from the Netherworld.**

Here's to you, babe.

—*THEA JAMES*

---

* Yes, his name is technically spelled "Betelgeuse," but to avoid confusion we'll stick with this informal spelling throughout.

** This spelling is used when referring to the film and the musical, while the animated series uses "Neitherworld."

TABLE OF CONTENTS

4 BREAKFAST

18 APPETIZERS

42 MAINS

90 SNACKS

110 DRINKS

144 DESSERTS

Charles's Birdwatching
Breakfast, pg. 10.

BREAKFAST

6 The Big Adventure

8 Feeling Flat Omelet

10 Charles's Birdwatching Breakfast

12 No Feet Cloud Eggs

14 Post–Bio-Exorcism Smoothie

16 Avocado Toast With the Most

THE BIG ADVENTURE

While a household name today, the Tim Burton of 1985 was directing his first feature film—and we're celebrating it with the first entry in this otherwise macabre book of *Beetlejuice* eats. *Pee-wee's Big Adventure* was a smashing success and is notable for solidifying Burton's cache as a director (and Danny Elfman's as a composer), directly leading to their incredible work on *Beetlejuice* in 1988. To fuel his big adventure, Pee-wee sits down to a big, very on-brand breakfast: pancake, egg eyes, strawberry nose and sausage mouth. Now you can do the same (Mr. T cereal topping optional).

SERVINGS 4 • PREP TIME 20 MINUTES • COOK TIME 20 MINUTES

INGREDIENTS

8 slices bacon

PANCAKES/FACE
1 cup all-purpose flour
1 Tbsp sugar
2 tsp baking powder
1 tsp baking soda
¼ tsp salt
3 Tbsp butter, divided
1 cup whole milk
1 large egg
1 tsp vanilla

BOILED EGGS/EYES
4 large eggs

NOSE
2 strawberries, halved

SAUSAGE/MOUTH
4 pork breakfast sausages

CEREAL/HAIR
2 cups shredded wheat cereal, optional

DIRECTIONS

❶ Preheat the oven to 375 degrees F.

❷ Line a baking sheet with parchment paper. Place the bacon in a single layer on the parchment paper and cook in oven for 5 to 7 minutes on each side or until browned and crispy. Drain on a paper towel. Set aside.

❸ In a medium bowl, mix together the flour, sugar, baking powder, baking soda and salt. Melt 2 Tbsp of butter in the microwave. In a separate bowl, mix together the milk, egg and vanilla. Mix the wet ingredients into the dry ingredients until just combined (don't overmix). Mix in butter. Let rest for 5 minutes.

❹ Bring a medium pot of water to a boil. Place 4 eggs into the boiling water and cook for 6 minutes. Remove with a slotted spoon and drain on a paper towel. Once the eggs are cool enough to handle, carefully remove the shells.

❺ In a non-stick pan, cook sausage on medium heat until browned on all sides.

❻ In a large non-stick skillet, melt the remaining butter. Place the batter into the pan to make 4 large pancakes; flip when bubbles appear on the tops. Cook for another couple of minutes or until cooked through.

❼ Place one pancake on each plate. Cut the bacon in half. Beneath each pancake, arrange the pieces in an X to resemble crossbones. Slice the eggs in half and set an egg onto each pancake to resemble eyes. Place strawberry halves in the center of each pancake to resemble a nose. Place a sausage onto each pancake to resemble a mouth. If desired, place an even amount of cereal on top to resemble hair.

FEELING FLAT OMELET

C onfused and looking for answers, Barbara and Adam Maitland turn to the *Handbook for the Recently Deceased* and hightail it to the Netherworld. Here, the couple is informed they're going to burn one of their three (per 125 years) class-one "help" intercessions with their caseworker, Juno, by appearing without an appointment. Shaken but determined, Barb and Adam wait patiently for Juno and are rewarded with a messenger who escorts them to the correct hall. Affectionately known as "Road Kill Man" by fans, this particular civil servant earned his name because he appears to have been run over by some very large cars in his final moments of life (not to worry, though; Road Kill Man totally owns his flatness). This intentionally messy dish, drenched with bloody hot sauce and balsamic glaze tire marks, is a salute to this Neitherworld hero.

SERVINGS 4 • **PREP TIME** 12 MINUTES • **COOK TIME** 8 MINUTES

INGREDIENTS

8 eggs	¼ tsp freshly ground black pepper
2 Tbsp chopped chives	1 Tbsp butter
½ cup grated sharp cheddar cheese	1 tomato, thinly sliced
½ tsp salt	2-8 dashes hot sauce
	Balsamic glaze, for drizzling

DIRECTIONS

❶ In a large bowl, whisk eggs until light and fluffy. Mix in the chives, cheese, salt and pepper.

❷ Set the oven to broil.

❸ On medium heat, melt the butter in a 10-inch oven-safe non-stick skillet.

❹ Pour in the egg mixture and top with the sliced tomatoes. Cook on medium heat for about 3 to 4 minutes. Place the pan in the oven and cook for another 3 to 4 minutes or until eggs are set and the tomatoes have a slight char.

❺ Slide the flat omelet onto a serving platter, top with hot sauce and drizzle with balsamic glaze (to resemble tire marks).

CHARLES'S BIRDWATCHING BREAKFAST

After an implied meltdown at his real estate job in Manhattan, Charles Deetz is a man on a mission. First, he needs to buy the Maitlands' quaint Connecticut home, trading in big city comforts for country air and small-town life. Then, seemingly hell-bent on wearing every cable-knit wool sweater emblazoned with birds he can find, Charles isolates in his new office, picks up a pair of binoculars and a copy of Audubon's *The Birds of America* and tries to embrace his role as an amateur ornithologist. This seed-forward breakfast bar, inspired by Charles's newfound hobby, is high in protein and guaranteed to fortify the most patient of bird-watchers.

SERVINGS 10 • **PREP TIME** 15 MINUTES • **COOK TIME** 1 HOUR

INGREDIENTS

- ½ cup sesame seeds
- ½ cup pistachios
- ½ cup flax seeds
- ½ cup pumpkin seeds
- ⅓ cup chopped dried dates
- ½ cup unsweetened shaved coconut
- ¼ cup raw organic honey
- 1 Tbsp coconut sugar
- 1 Tbsp olive oil

DIRECTIONS

❶ In a dry frying pan on medium heat, toast all the seeds and nuts separately until each is lightly toasted.

❷ In a bowl, mix together the nuts, seeds, dates and coconut.

❸ In a small saucepan on medium-low heat, warm the honey and sugar together until the sugar has melted. Pour the honey into the bowl and stir to coat all the ingredients.

❹ Line a 10½-by-6-inch pan with parchment paper and brush all sides with oil.

❺ Place mixture in pan and press ingredients down tightly, making an even thickness. Cover with another piece of parchment paper brushed with oil and press parchment against the mixture. Place in the refrigerator to set for at least 1 hour.

❻ Take out of the refrigerator and cut into 10 even bars.

NO FEET CLOUD EGGS

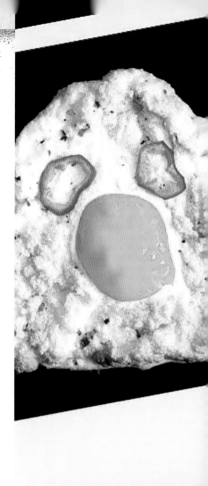

A fter their first encounter with Juno, their afterlife caseworker, Barbara and Adam are encouraged to take care of their pesky living housemates themselves. Haunting is covered in the *Handbook for the Recently Deceased*, after all. But when their first attempt at spooking the newcomers doesn't have the desired effect (it's no use pulling off your face if the living can't see you), the couple decides to go old school, draping themselves in sheets and moaning to get the attention of the Deetz family. Armed with her Polaroid camera, Lydia Deetz catches the pair on film and notices, to her shock, that the people wearing the sheets are floating—no feet. This fluffy egg recipe, inspired by the Maitlands' pathetic attempt at a haunting, actually is a breakfast you'll want to eat for the next 125 years.

SERVINGS 4 • **PREP TIME** 9 MINUTES • **COOK TIME** 6 MINUTES

INGREDIENTS

- 4 large eggs
- 1 Tbsp olive oil
- 2 Tbsp chopped fresh chives, divided
- ½ cup finely grated Gruyere cheese
- ¼ tsp salt
- ¼ tsp freshly ground pepper
- 2 mini red peppers, sliced into rounds
- 2 slices cooked crisp bacon, crumbled

DIRECTIONS

❶ Preheat the oven to 450 degrees F.

❷ Separate the eggs carefully, keeping the yolks intact.

❸ Line a baking sheet with parchment paper. Brush the parchment paper with olive oil.

❹ Place the egg whites into a mixing bowl and beat to form stiff peaks. Carefully fold in 1 Tbsp chives, cheese, salt and pepper. Place 4 even mounds of the egg whites onto the baking sheet into 4 ghost shapes. Add 2 pepper slices to each ghost for eyes. Make an indent in the egg whites below the eyes.

❺ Place in the oven for 3 minutes. Remove and carefully place the egg yolks into the indents to form a mouth. Place back into the oven and cook for another 3 minutes. Remove from the oven and garnish with the remaining chives and bacon.

Safe and Simple Separating

Yolks are no joke, folks. The best way to handle them? Well, by hand! To separate from the egg whites, gently cup your fingers under the yolk and lift.

POST-BIO-EXORCISM
SMOOTHIE

One of the endearing things about *Beetlejuice* is the number of ridiculous puns and slapstick jokes throughout the film. Take, for example, the titular ghoul's chosen profession as a bio-exorcist, zoned for commercial, industrial and residential removal of living pests who plague the dead. The 1989-1991 animated *Beetlejuice* television series takes puns to the extreme (each episode is a nearly endless barrage of audio-visual quips)—for example, when Lydia asks BJ if he'd like to work out, Beetlejuice replies, "I've exorcised enough!" Inspired by Beetlejuice's exorcism schedule, this smoothie should sustain its drinker straight on through the afterlife.

SERVINGS 1-2 • **PREP TIME** 3 MINUTES

INGREDIENTS

- 1 ripe banana
- ¼ cup natural peanut butter (no sugar added)
- 1 cup blueberries, divided
- ½ cup unsweetened cashew or unsweetened Greek yogurt
- 1 ½ cup unsweetened almond milk
- 1 tsp vanilla extract
- 4 slices kiwi
- 4 blackberries

DIRECTIONS

❶ Place the banana, peanut butter, ¾ of the blueberries, yogurt, almond milk and vanilla extract into a blender and blend until smooth.

❷ Pour into 2 glasses and garnish each with kiwi slices, blackberries and the remaining blueberries.

Smooth Substitutions

Tallying your banana intake? Allergic to peanuts? Feel free to substitute any of these ingredients to make this smoothie more to your liking.

AVOCADO TOAST WITH THE MOST

Lydia Deetz's first conversation with Beetlejuice occurs when she finds a teeny-tiny version of the self-proclaimed "Ghost with the Most" camping out in the scale model of Winter River in the attic. Lydia wants to join the land of the dead, Beetlejuice wants to return to the land of the living, and so they settle for a game of charades, prompting Lydia to try to guess his name and say it three times. After some trial and error ("orange beetle," "beetle fruit," "beetle drink"), Lydia gets there, but wisely holds back from saying the name a third time. Smashed avo toast with orange juice (hold the beetle) need not require the same restraint, though—the more avocado, the merrier.

SERVINGS 4 • **PREP TIME** 15 MINUTES • **COOK TIME** 20 MINUTES

INGREDIENTS

- 1 sweet potato, thinly sliced
- 1 Tbsp olive oil
- ¼ tsp salt
- ¼ tsp freshly ground pepper
- 4 eggs
- 2 avocados
- 1 Tbsp fresh lemon juice
- 4 slices sprouted grain bread
- 1 tsp everything bagel seasoning
- ⅓ cup microgreens

DIRECTIONS

❶ Preheat the oven to 375 degrees F.

❷ Place the potato slices on a parchment-lined baking sheet, drizzle with oil and season with salt and pepper. Mix to coat, then place potatoes in the oven and cook for about 15 to 20 minutes or until tender.

❸ Bring a large, shallow pot of water to a gentle boil. In a small fine sieve over a sink or bowl, break the eggs open one at a time and let the runny part of the egg drain out. Stir the water before sliding the eggs into the water. Cook the eggs for 2 to 3 minutes or until eggs are set but yolk is still runny. Remove eggs with a slotted spoon and drain on a paper towel.

❹ In a small bowl, mash the avocados with a fork, then stir in lemon juice.

❺ Toast the bread to a golden brown.

❻ Place the toast on a serving platter. Top each evenly with potatoes, then avocado mash, then one egg. Sprinkle the everything bagel seasoning on top and garnish evenly with microgreens.

Open Season(ing)

If you don't fancy everything bagel seasoning—or you'd like to top this toast with something more tailor-made—try avocado toast seasoning!

Jane's Buttered Buns,
pg. 26.

APPETIZERS

20 Sandworm Soft Pretzels With Cheddar-Beer Sauce

22 Eek! Salad

24 (Un)Holy Guacamole

26 Jane's Buttered Buns

28 Dante's Inferno Hot Wings

30 Jacques LaLean's French Onion Soup

32 Candy (Pop)corn

34 Charred Corn on the Cob

36 Showstopper Shrimp Cocktail

38 Manhattan Hand Rolls

40 Deviled Eggs

SANDWORM
SOFT PRETZELS WITH
CHEDDAR-BEER SAUCE

At the climax of the movie, Beetlejuice is on the brink of freedom from the Netherworld thanks to his plan to marry Lydia Deetz (against her will). Enter Barbara Maitland, riding an enormous sandworm who scarfs down The Ghost with the Most in one fell swoop. These sandworm-esque soft pretzels, with accompanying cheddar-beer dip, pay homage to the scene. Consuming them in one bite is at the eater's discretion, as is the type of pretzels you choose to incorporate into the dip as a topper (e.g., jalapeño ranch, which adds a delightful kick alongside the crunch).

MAKES 20 PRETZELS • **PREP TIME** 1½ HOURS • **COOK TIME** 20 MINUTES

INGREDIENTS

PRETZELS
- ¼ cup light brown sugar
- 1½ cups warm water (100-110 degrees F)
- 1 (¼-oz) envelope active dry yeast
- ¼ cup olive oil, plus more for greasing
- 3¾ cups all-purpose flour, plus more for kneading
- ½ cup baking soda
- ¼ cup black sesame seeds
- ¼ cup coarse salt

CHEDDAR-BEER DIP
- 3 Tbsp butter
- 3 Tbsp flour
- ½ cup pale ale
- 1½ cups whole milk
- ½ tsp salt
- ½ tsp freshly ground black pepper
- 1 tsp Dijon mustard
- ¼ tsp paprika
- 2 Tbsp hot sauce
- 1 tsp Worcestershire sauce
- 2 cups shredded sharp cheddar cheese
- 1 cup shredded habanero cheddar cheese
- ½ cup crushed store-bought pretzels

DIRECTIONS

❶ In a large bowl, stir the brown sugar into 1½ cups of warm water until dissolved. Sprinkle the yeast over the water and let stand until foamy, about 5 minutes. Stir in the oil and flour.

❷ On a work surface with a dusting of flour, knead the dough until silky. Add more flour if too sticky. Place dough into a bowl that has been greased with olive oil. Cover with a clean kitchen towel and set in a draft-free area until the dough has doubled in size (about 45 minutes).

❸ Line 2 baking sheets with parchment paper and brush paper with oil.

❹ Punch down the dough and place on a floured work surface. Flatten the dough and cut into 20 equal pieces, then form into 5-to-6-inch sticks. Place the sticks onto the baking sheets. Let rise for 20 minutes.

❺ Preheat the oven to 450 degrees F.

❻ In a large shallow skillet with enough water to cover pretzel sticks, stir in baking soda and bring to a simmer.

Place the sticks carefully into the water and cook for 30 seconds (cook in batches to not overcrowd the pan), then remove and place back onto the baking sheets. Curve each pretzel in an S shape. Sprinkle with black sesame seeds and salt to create black and white sandworm stripes.

7 Place on the bottom rack of the oven and bake for about 12 minutes or until browned.

8 In a medium saucepan on medium-low heat, melt the butter. Whisk in the flour and cook for 1 minute, stirring continuously. Add in the beer and cook for another minute, whisking often. Slowly add in milk while whisking so lumps don't form.

9 Season with salt, pepper, mustard, paprika, hot sauce and Worcestershire sauce. Bring the sauce to a slight simmer, stir in the cheese and cook until the cheese has melted. Place the sauce in a serving bowl and top with the crushed pretzels to resemble sand.

EEK! SALAD

After arriving in Winter River, Connecticut, avant-garde artist Delia Deetz and her professional yes-man, Otho Fenlock, begin aggressively investigating and planning a remodel of the new Deetz family abode. Opening all the doors in the house and evaluating each of the rooms (complete with admittedly dowdy wallpaper and country catalog-ready home decor), Otho snidely asks to be saved from L.L. Bean. This bean salad is heavy on the vinegar to match Otho and Delia's acerbic attitudes.

SERVINGS 4-6 • **PREP TIME** 12 MINUTES

INGREDIENTS

- 2 (15-oz) cans cannellini beans, rinsed and drained
- 1 Tbsp chopped fresh parsley
- ¼ cup diced roasted red pepper
- 2 Tbsp chopped fresh chives
- ⅓ cup olive oil
- 2 Tbsp apple cider vinegar
- Juice and zest of 1 lemon
- ½ tsp salt
- ⅛ tsp freshly ground black pepper
- Chive flowers for garnish, if available

DIRECTIONS

❶ In a large bowl, mix together the beans, parsley, red peppers and chives.

❷ Place the olive oil, vinegar, lemon zest and juice, salt and pepper into a jar with a lid and shake until combined. Pour over the bean mixture and toss to coat.

❸ Garnish with chive flowers and serve with your favorite crackers or crostini.

(UN)HOLY GUACAMOLE

While checking out the business (aka obituary) section in the morning paper, Beetlejuice singles out Adam and Barbara Maitland as a cute, probably gullible couple. During an attempt to win their bio-exorcism business, Beetlejuice is asked to provide his qualifications, which he rattles off to impressive effect. Though he's a self-proclaimed attendee of Julliard, graduate of the Harvard Business School, survivor of the Black Plague and current bio-exorcist, Beetlejuice is singularly proud of the fact that he's seen *The Exorcist* 167 times. Inspired by the bio-exorcist's love of the classic horror film, this guac recipe is reminiscent of Linda Blair's exceptional projectile performance.

SERVINGS 4 • **PREP TIME** 10 MINUTES

INGREDIENTS

4 avocados	1 Tbsp chopped fresh cilantro
¼ tsp ground cumin	3 Tbsp fresh lime juice
⅓ cup deseeded and diced tomato	1 tsp hot pepper sauce
¼ cup minced red onion	¼ tsp salt
1 jalapeño, deseeded and minced	¼ tsp freshly ground pepper
	1 coconut, optional

DIRECTIONS

❶ Mash avocados into a chunky consistency. Stir in the remaining ingredients.

❷ Cut a wide hole in the coconut for the mouth. Draw Xs for eyes to complete the scary coconut face. Arrange the guacamole so it's coming out of the mouth.

JANE'S BUTTERED BUNS

B arbara Maitland's cousin, Jane Butterfield, is a real piece of work. A persistent real estate agent and aspiring home decorator, Jane has been showing pictures of her cousin's house to Manhattanite investors on the sly, despite Barbara and Adam's repeated refusal to sell. On her latest attempt to convince her cousin, Jane tells Barbara she has a big city bidder who has offered $260,000 for the house—while also sneaking in a comment about the Maitlands' lack of offspring. These buttered buns are a nod to Jane Butterfield's tenacity as well as her tone-deafness.

SERVINGS 4-6 • **PREP TIME** 1½ HOURS
COOK TIME 20 MINUTES

INGREDIENTS

BUNS

- 3½ cups all-purpose flour, plus more for kneading
- 2 (¼-oz) packets instant yeast
- 1 tsp salt
- 1 cup warm water (between 100-110 degrees F)
- ⅓ cup whole milk, room temperature
- ¼ cup salted butter, melted, plus more for greasing bowl and skillet

GARLIC-HERB BUTTER

- 4 Tbsp salted butter
- 1 tsp chopped fresh parsley
- ¼ tsp chopped fresh rosemary
- ½ tsp fresh thyme
- 1 tsp chopped fresh basil
- 1 clove garlic, minced
- ½ tsp salt
- ¼ tsp freshly ground pepper

DIRECTIONS

❶ In a large mixing bowl, mix together the flour, yeast and salt. Add in the warm water, milk and butter. Mix until combined, place on a work surface and knead dough until smooth. Place the dough in a large bowl that has been greased with butter and flip dough around to coat. Place in a draft-free area covered with a clean kitchen towel. Let the dough rise until doubled in size (about 45 minutes).

❷ In a small saucepan, melt the butter and add the fresh herbs, garlic, salt and pepper. Set aside.

❸ Grease a 10-inch cast iron skillet with butter. Form the dough into 12 equal balls. Place the dough balls around the edge of the skillet and in a circle in the middle. Place in a draft-free area covered with a clean kitchen towel and let rise for 20 minutes.

❹ Preheat the oven to 400 degrees F.

❺ Brush the tops with half of the garlic-herb butter. Bake for about 30 minutes or until lightly golden brown and cooked through. Remove from oven and brush with remaining garlic-herb butter before serving.

DANTE'S INFERNO
HOT WINGS

After first appearing to the Deetz family, Beetlejuice (once again in Adam's model of Winter River) gets a stern talking-to by the Maitlands, who are upset with his tactics. Barbara gets even more upset when Beetlejuice makes some sleazy remarks about Lydia Deetz (whom he refers to as "Edgar Allan Poe's daughter"), and asks the Maitlands where an ordinary guy like him could work out some of his...dating anxiety (it's been 600 years since his last paramour). And that's when he sees it: Dante's Inferno Room. Boasting GIRLS GIRLS GIRLS and free AC, along with a bitchin' sound system and spectacular lighting effects, Dante's Inferno doesn't really fit in with the rest of Adam's meticulously groomed model town (and he of course denies building it). This chicken wing recipe is best served the way Dante recommends: HOT HOT HOT.

SERVINGS 4-6 • **PREP TIME** 15 MINUTES • **COOK TIME** 20 MINUTES

INGREDIENTS

INFERNO WING SAUCE
- 1 stick salted butter
- ¾ cup hot sauce
- 1 clove garlic, smashed
- 1 tsp cayenne pepper
- 1 tsp red pepper flakes
- 1 jalapeño pepper, chopped
- 1 Carolina reaper pepper, chopped while wearing gloves

COOLING WING DIP
- 2 Tbsp minced English cucumber
- ½ cup blue cheese crumbles
- ½ cup sour cream
- ¼ cup mayonnaise
- 1 Tbsp milk
- 1 Tbsp freshly squeezed lemon juice
- ¼ tsp salt
- ⅛ tsp freshly ground black pepper

WINGS
- 1 cup all-purpose flour
- ½ tsp salt
- ½ tsp freshly ground black pepper
- 1 Tbsp cayenne pepper
  Oil for frying
- 2 lb chicken wing drumettes

DIRECTIONS

❶ Wearing gloves, place all the wing sauce ingredients in a medium saucepan. Heat the ingredients until the butter melts, then carefully transfer into a blender and blend until smooth. Pour through a fine mesh sieve back into the saucepan. Bring the mixture to a simmer and cook for about 5 minutes to meld the flavors and thicken the sauce.

❷ In a bowl, mix all cooling wing dip ingredients and refrigerate.

❸ Mix the flour, salt, black pepper and cayenne in a shallow bowl. Place the wings into the mixture and toss to coat.

❹ Bring the oil to 350 degrees F and cook the wings in batches until golden brown and cooked through (8 to 10 minutes). Coat each wing in wing sauce. Serve with dip.

Proper Pepper Handling

Carolina reaper peppers are no joke. Be sure to wear gloves when handling these, and avoid touching your eyes!

JACQUES LALEAN'S FRENCH ONION SOUP

T he animated *Beetlejuice* series from the 1990s introduces a number of new faces not seen in the film, including Jacques LaLean, Beetlejuice's skeleton friend. An aspiring bodybuilder, the Frenchman LaLean—named for real-world bodybuilder Jack LaLanne—serves as cartoon comedic relief (BJ is quite fond of knocking Jacques to pieces or siccing the dogs on him). This loaded French onion soup gets its flavor from simmering broth with, what else? Bones.

SERVINGS 4 • **PREP TIME** 15 MINUTES • **COOK TIME** 30 MINUTES

INGREDIENTS

- 1 Tbsp olive oil
- 1 Tbsp salted butter
- 5 yellow onions, thinly sliced
- 2 Tbsp all-purpose flour
- ¼ cup dry white wine
- 1 Tbsp dry sherry
- 6 cups beef stock
- ½ tsp herbes de Provence
- 4 (¾-inch) slices French baguette, toasted
- 1½ cups grated Gruyère cheese

DIRECTIONS

❶ In a large Dutch oven, add oil and butter. Add onions and mix to coat. Cook on medium-low heat for 15 to 20 minutes, stirring often. Stir in the flour and cook for another 1 to 2 minutes. Whisk in the white wine and sherry, then cook for another minute. Slowly whisk in stock and season with herbes de Provence. Bring to a simmer and cook for 10 minutes.

❷ Preheat the oven to broil.

❸ Pour soup evenly into 4 bowls. Place a slice of toasted baguette onto each, then top evenly with Gruyère. Place the bowls on a baking sheet and put on the middle rack of the oven. Cook (watching carefully) until cheese is melted and slightly browned.

Ace in the Bowl

While any old bowl will do, you might want to invest in the likes of lion's head bowls if you plan to make this dish often. These deep porcelain bowls hold large portions and are frequently used for French onion soup.

CANDY (POP)CORN

After distracting Beetlejuice with Dante's Inferno Room (see Dante's Inferno Hot Wings, pg. 28), the Maitlands find themselves transported back to the Netherworld and in the presence of their caseworker, Juno. (Turns out it was Juno, not Adam, who had the idea for the adult entertainment.) Juno's office is also the scene of a pretty cool Easter egg, in which a Day-Glo moviegoing audience is visible behind Barbara and Adam. This optical illusion creates a kind of Burton-esque mirror: members of the *Beetlejuice*-watching audience are face to face with Netherworld inhabitants who also appear to be watching a movie and chowing down on snacks. Snacks like this "bloody" caramel popcorn, of course.

SERVINGS 4 • **PREP TIME** 5 MINUTES • **COOK TIME** 6 MINUTES

INGREDIENTS

- ½ cup red chocolate melts
- 3 Tbsp vegetable oil
- ½ cup popcorn kernels
- ¼ cup prepared caramel
- 1 Tbsp sea salt

DIRECTIONS

❶ In a double boiler, melt the chocolate.

❷ In a heavy-bottomed pot with a lid, add oil and popcorn kernels. On medium-high heat, pop the kernels by shaking the pot. Cook until the popping slows down. Remove from heat and wait until popping stops.

❸ Pour the popcorn into a bowl, pour half of the melted chocolate and all of the caramel and sea salt into the bowl and toss to coat. Drizzle the remaining chocolate over the popcorn.

CHARRED CORN ON THE COB

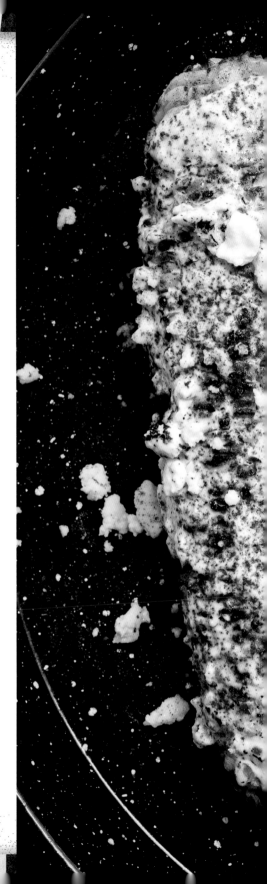

When Barbara and Adam first make their way to Netherworld, they find themselves in a heavily populated waiting room. While the bureaucracy of the afterlife is certainly unexpected, the Maitlands find themselves equally taken aback by the waiting room's inhabitants. One particular denizen is a rather well-done smoker/burn victim affectionately nicknamed Char Man by fans. This charred corn on the cob recipe resembles the crispy character—particularly if you accidentally leave the corn on the grill a little too long.

SERVINGS 4 • **PREP TIME** 7 MINUTES • **COOK TIME** 7 MINUTES

INGREDIENTS

4 ears corn	½ tsp salt
¼ cup mayonnaise	½ ground black pepper
¼ cup sour cream	½ cup finely crumbled cotija cheese
1 Tbsp fresh lime juice	
1 small clove garlic, minced	½ tsp paprika
½ tsp cumin	

DIRECTIONS

❶ Preheat the grill to medium-high heat.

❷ Remove the husk and silk from the corn.

❸ In a medium bowl, mix together the mayonnaise, sour cream, lime juice, garlic, cumin, salt and pepper.

❹ Brush each piece of corn with half of the mayonnaise mixture. Place the corn onto the preheated grill and cook for about 7 to 10 minutes or until the corn is slightly charred on all sides.

❺ Remove the corn from the grill and brush evenly with the remaining mayonnaise mixture. Cover each evenly with the crumbled cotija cheese and paprika.

SHOWSTOPPER SHRIMP COCKTAIL

Delia Deetz has invested a lot of time and energy into her new home. She didn't want to move to middle-of-nowhere Connecticut, but humoring her husband's need to embrace small-town life, she doubles down on the situation in an effort to make the house fit her singular artistic vision. This includes throwing a dinner party for the couple's old Manhattan friends and serving a magnificent (if unexpected) home-cooked meal. This shrimp cocktail is Delia's first dinner party dish, guaranteed to make you belt out Belafonte. Note: Visual preparation is key for this dish. Making the shrimp cocktail look as hand-like as possible is recommended for maximum effect.

SERVINGS 4 • **PREP TIME** 10 MINUTES • **COOK TIME** 4 MINUTES

INGREDIENTS

GRILLED BLACKENED SHRIMP COCKTAIL
- 20 large shrimp
- 2 Tbsp blackened seasoning

BLACK GARLIC AIOLI
- 1 cup mayonnaise
- 1 lemon, juiced
- ½ Tbsp Dijon mustard
- ¼ tsp salt
- 4 cloves black garlic

DIRECTIONS

❶ Preheat the grill to medium.

❷ Peel the shrimp from the shell, leaving the tails attached. Place a skewer through each shrimp and season evenly with blackened seasoning. Place the shrimp onto the preheated grill and cook for 2 minutes on each side or until the shrimp turn pink.

❸ Meanwhile, in a blender, blend the aioli ingredients until smooth.

❹ Pour aioli into 4 small bowls. Remove the skewers from the shrimp and add five shrimp to each bowl, tails pointing out. Arrange the shrimp to look like fingers by grouping 4 shrimp together and one shrimp farther apart to resemble a thumb.

MANHATTAN HAND ROLLS

U pon moving into his new house, Charles Deetz is annoyingly, incessantly optimistic. Confident that the place is perfect for his family and convinced that Winter River's quaintness will win over even his most jaded developer friends, Charles is eager to espouse the thrill of small-town life (and its marketability) via a fancy dinner party. For Delia, though, the dinner party is about a return to normalcy—and so she prepares meals guaranteed to impress. These Japanese-inspired hand rolls are both era-appropriate (the '80s saw an embrace of Japanese food and culture in America) and on-brand for Delia (hand rolls resemble some of her sculptures).

MAKES 24 HAND ROLLS • **PREP TIME** 15 MINUTES

INGREDIENTS

- 4 nori sheets
- 2 cups cooked black rice
- 1 lb sushi-grade ahi tuna, cut into ½-inch cubes
- 1 Tbsp black sesame seeds
- 2 avocados, pitted and sliced
- 3 Tbsp soy sauce
- ¼ cup sour cream
- 4 Tbsp black roe caviar

DIRECTIONS

❶ Cut the nori sheets into 3½-by-2-inch pieces, making 24 pieces. Bend each like a taco shell, place an even amount of rice onto each and top with an even amount of tuna. Evenly sprinkle sesame seeds and place a slice of avocado on top.

❷ In a small bowl, mix the soy sauce and sour cream together. Drizzle each hand roll with the sauce and top with caviar.

DEVILED EGGS

Delia Deetz is no pushover. She's prickly, determined and (most importantly) has a vision for her house and standard of living, even if her husband has whisked her away from her life in New York. Prepping for what becomes an infamous dinner party, Delia appears to be making enough vegetables for a small army (see Manhattan Hand Rolls, pg. 38) and has a stern talk with her morose stepdaughter, Lydia. Delia might be shrill, demanding and devoid of patience for anyone who gets in her way, but she's also got a killer sense of style and a desire to be at the cutting edge—this applies to her cuisine, as well. These creatively colored deviled eggs absolutely belong on Delia's dress-to-impress/single-glove-clad dinner menu.

MAKES 12 DEVILED EGGS • **PREP TIME** 15 MINUTES • **COOK TIME** 11 MINUTES

INGREDIENTS

- 6 eggs
- ⅓ cup mayonnaise
- ½ cup Greek yogurt
- ½ Tbsp Dijon mustard
- ½ avocado
- 1 Tbsp chopped fresh dill
- 1 Tbsp chopped fresh parsley
- 1 Tbsp chopped fresh basil
- 1 Tbsp chopped chives
- ½ lemon, juiced
- 1 clove garlic
- ¼ tsp salt
- ¼ tsp freshly ground black pepper
- 12 large green olives

DIRECTIONS

❶ Place eggs in a medium pot of water and bring to a boil. Cover the pot with a lid, turn off the heat and let the eggs sit for 11 minutes. Drain hot water and fill the pot with cold water and ice cubes to cool.

❷ Once the eggs are cool, remove the shells. Cut each egg in half lengthwise. Scoop out the yolks and place into a food processor or blender. Add remaining ingredients except olives and blend until smooth. Pipe the mixture evenly into the egg halves.

❸ Cut each olive into 4 slices. Stand the olives up in the outer edge of the filling of each egg, curving them in.

It's All Good, Bro
Fish Tacos, pg. 62.

MAINS

44 14½-Minute Chops

46 Beetlejuice Goes Hawaiian

48 By the Handbook Roasted Turkey

50 Chicken Noodle Soup

52 It's Chowtime! Chow Mein

54 Chop Top's Steak Tips

56 Disembodied Spatchcocked Chicken

58 Everything But the Kitchen Sink Pasta

60 I'm Stuffed Bone-In Chicken Breast

62 It's All Good, Bro Fish Tacos

64 Keaton's Ad-Libbed Taco Bar

66 Maitland Meatloaf

68 Fancy Pants Lobster Mac and Cheese

70 Miss Argentina Flank Steak

72 Neitherworld Picnic Spread

74 Orange (Juice) Chicken

76 Orion's Betelgeuse Burger

78 Party Like a Roman Rack of Lamb

80 Scared Sheetless Sheet Pan Fajitas

82 Sesame Broiled Salmon

84 Juno's Smoked Brisket

86 The Cal Worthington Special

88 Till Death Do Us Part Spaghetti and Meatballs

14½-MINUTE CHOPS

Fun fact: Michael Keaton wasn't Tim Burton's initial choice for Beetlejuice (that would be Sammy Davis Jr., followed by Arnold Schwarzenegger). But after agreeing to the role, it was Keaton who had the idea of Beetlejuice's overall look, including his used car salesman persona, electric-shock hair and moldy skin. Appearing on screen for a scant 14½ minutes of the 90-minute movie, Keaton delivers an absolutely show-stopping performance, showcasing his comedic chops while devouring the scenery. Speaking of hamming it up and chowing down, this pork chop recipe can be prepared in less than 20 minutes and is as memorable as Keaton's incredible character work.

SERVINGS 4 • **PREP TIME** 4½ MINUTES
COOK TIME 10 MINUTES

INGREDIENTS

PORK CHOPS
- 4 (8-oz) bone-in pork chops
- ½ tsp salt
- ¼ tsp freshly ground pepper
- ½ cup all-purpose flour
- 2 Tbsp oil

SAGE CREAM SAUCE
- 2 Tbsp butter
- 6 fresh sage leaves
- ½ cup chicken broth
- ½ cup heavy cream
- ¼ tsp salt
- ¼ tsp freshly ground pepper

DIRECTIONS

❶ Season the pork chops on both sides with salt and pepper. Coat each pork chop with flour. In a large nonstick skillet with oil over medium-high heat, cook chops for about 3 minutes (depending on thickness) on each side or until internal temperature reaches

145 degrees F. Remove from skillet and let rest for 5 to 7 minutes.

❷ In the same pan, on medium-low heat, add the butter and sage leaves and cook until leaves are crispy. Remove and set aside.

❸ In the same pan, stir in the broth, cream, salt and pepper. Cook until thickened. Pour sauce over pork, then crush fried sage leaves and sprinkle on top.

BEETLEJUICE GOES HAWAIIAN

A sequel to *Beetlejuice* has been on the table since 1990, when Tim Burton hired Jonathan Gems to write a film combining Beetlejuice, surfing and German Expressionism. The name of that unproduced sequel? *Beetlejuice Goes Hawaiian*. Unfortunately for BJ fans, Burton and Keaton were hard at work on the Batman films and couldn't make *Hawaiian* a reality—though more than three decades later, it looks like there's hope for a Keaton-Ryder-Burton sequel. While it's unlikely the original Aloha State theme will hold, these kebabs pay homage to what might have been.

SERVINGS 4–6 • **PREP TIME** 42 MINUTES • **COOK TIME** 10 MINUTES

INGREDIENTS

SAUCE
- ½ cup ketchup
- ¼ cup low-sodium soy sauce
- ¼ cup pineapple juice
- 2 Tbsp brown sugar
- 1 inch fresh ginger, peeled and grated
- 2 cloves garlic, minced

KEBABS
- 2 lb cooked ham
- 1 can pineapple, drained
- 1 red onion
- 2 red peppers

DIRECTIONS

❶ If using wooden skewers, soak skewers in water for about 30 minutes before using.

❷ In a nonstick pot, whisk all sauce ingredients together. Bring to a simmer and cook until thickened (about 5 to 7 minutes).

❸ Preheat the grill to medium heat.

❹ Cut the ham and pineapple into 1-inch squares; slice the onion and peppers into 1-inch slices. Thread ham, pineapple, onions and peppers onto skewers. Repeat order until skewers are full.

❺ Brush skewers with sauce and place onto grill. Cook until the sauce has caramelized on all sides, brushing on more as it cooks (about 10 minutes).

❻ Remove from the grill. Serve as kebabs or over rice if desired.

BY THE HANDBOOK ROASTED TURKEY

A prominent presence throughout *Beetlejuice* is the *Handbook for the Recently Deceased,* which magically appears in the Maitland living room upon the drowned couple's return to their home. Both Barb and Adam give up trying to read the book closely early on—per Adam, the thing reads like stereo instructions—and instead take a more trial-and-error approach to the afterlife. As the Maitlands soon discover from their very first trip to the Netherworld, however, the *Handbook* is actually kind of a huge deal. Its instructions need to be followed to the letter or calamity ensues—not unlike a traditional Thanksgiving roasted turkey recipe, which requires constant attention and careful adherence to instructions to avoid a dried-out or undercooked bird.

SERVINGS 4–6 • **PREP TIME** 20 MINUTES • **COOK TIME** 2 HOURS 30 MINUTES

INGREDIENTS

TURKEY
- 1 stick butter, room temperature
- 1 Tbsp chopped fresh sage
- 1 tsp chopped fresh rosemary
- 1 tsp chopped fresh thyme
- ¼ tsp salt
- ¼ tsp freshly ground pepper
- 1 (11–13-lb) turkey

GRAVY
- 1 onion, peeled and roughly chopped
- 2 stalks celery
- 2 carrots
- 1 small bunch fresh sage, divided
- 1 small bunch fresh rosemary, divided
- 1 small bunch fresh thyme, divided
- 6 cups chicken broth, divided
- ¼ cup butter
- ¼ cup flour

DIRECTIONS

❶ Preheat the oven to 325 degrees F.

❷ In a small bowl, mix butter, herbs, salt and pepper. Carefully loosen the skin from the meat of the turkey breasts. Place half the butter mixture under the skin and half onto the skin.

❸ Place the onion, celery and carrots on the bottom of a roasting pan, then add in half of the herbs, pour a cup of broth into the bottom and place turkey on top of vegetables and herbs. Place into the preheated oven and cook until the internal temperature reaches 160 degrees F (about 2 hours and 30 minutes), basting turkey with broth as it cooks. If the turkey becomes too brown, tent with foil.

❹ In a saucepan, add remaining broth, remaining herbs and the turkey neck from the turkey giblets. Bring the gravy to a slow simmer and cover. Continue to simmer while the turkey cooks, adding water if needed.

❺ Remove turkey from oven, place on a cutting board and cover loosely with foil to rest for 30 minutes.

❻ Add all the drippings from the pan to the pot of gravy and continue to simmer. In another saucepan on medium-low heat, melt the butter, whisk in the flour and cook for 1 to 2 minutes. Place a strainer on the pot and pour the gravy into the pot, straining out all the other ingredients. Whisk, bring the gravy to a simmer to thicken and remove oil with a ladle. Serve with the turkey.

CHICKEN NOODLE SOUP

When Adam and Barbara first return home after drowning in their car, they find themselves cold, tired and completely disoriented. They find a copy of their afterlife manual, the *Handbook for the Recently Deceased*, which Adam originally mistakes for a *Handbook for the Recently Diseased*. Published by Handbook for the Recently Deceased Press, Barb and Adam quickly come to the realization that they are technically no longer living. Overwhelmed with the news of their demise (and the fact that they can never leave their house again), the Maitlands are in need of some comfort. When you feel as if you've died, nothing cures the "diseased" better than chicken noodle soup.

SERVINGS 4 • **PREP TIME** 15 MINUTES • **COOK TIME** 45 MINUTES

INGREDIENTS

- 4 large bone-in chicken thighs
- 2 Tbsp olive oil
- 2 carrots, sliced
- 2 celery stalks, sliced
- 1 onion, diced
- 2 cloves garlic, minced
- ¼ tsp salt
- ¼ tsp freshly ground pepper
- 8 cups chicken broth
- 9 oz wide egg noodles
- 2 Tbsp fresh parsley, chopped, optional

DIRECTIONS

❶ Preheat the oven to 350 degrees F.

❷ Place the chicken in a roasting pan and put in the oven, skin side up. Cook for 30 to 35 minutes or until internal temperature reaches 165 degrees F.

❸ In a large soup pot with olive oil on medium heat, cook the carrots, celery and onion for about 5 minutes, stirring occasionally. Add in the garlic and cook for another minute. Season with salt and pepper. Add the broth and bring to a simmer.

❹ Bring a pot of salted water to a boil. Cook noodles according to package directions.

❺ When the chicken is cooled enough to handle, remove the skin and fatty pieces and shred the chicken into bigger than bite-size pieces. Place shredded chicken into the pot.

❻ Place the desired amount of pasta into 4 serving bowls, top with soup and serve.

IT'S CHOWTIME!
CHOW MEIN

T heir first night in Winter River, Connecticut, the Deetz family does what most families do after a move: They order takeout. Passing around several cartons of delicious Chinese food, the Deetzes talk about their new home, their plans for the future and how happy (Charles, see Birdwatching Breakfast, pg. 10), indifferent (Lydia, see My Life Is One Big, Dark Chocolate Mousse, pg. 158) and upset (Delia, see The Prince Valium, pg. 136) they are with the house. Like all good takeout, this stir-fry recipe is guaranteed to bring even the most disparate family together.

SERVINGS 6 • **PREP TIME** 15 MINUTES • **COOK TIME** 10 MINUTES

INGREDIENTS

SAUCE
- ¼ cup low-sodium soy sauce
- 1 Tbsp sesame oil
- ⅓ cup chicken broth
- 1 Tbsp brown sugar
- 1 Tbsp cornstarch
- ½ tsp freshly ground black pepper

CHOW MEIN
- 12 oz chow mein broad noodles
- 1 lb boneless chicken breast
- 2 Tbsp olive oil
- 2 cups shredded green cabbage
- 1 stalk celery, thinly sliced
- 1 carrot, julienned
- ¼ cup chopped green onions

DIRECTIONS

❶ Mix all the sauce ingredients in a bowl and set aside.
❷ Cook noodles according to package directions.
❸ Cut chicken into small, thin slices. Heat a wok on medium-high heat. Add oil and cook chicken until lightly browned on all sides. Remove from the wok and set aside.

❹ Add in cabbage, celery and carrots and cook for about 2 minutes or until softened, stirring often.
❺ Stir in the sauce and cook until thickened. Add the chicken and noodles to the wok and toss to coat. Garnish with green onions.

CHOP TOP'S STEAK TIPS

One perhaps lesser-known inspiration for Michael Keaton's Beetlejuice is Robert "Chop Top" Sawyer, played by Bill Moseley, from the disturbing but also hilarious *The Texas Chainsaw Massacre 2*. A macabre fast-talking murderer, Chop Top gives bio-exorcist scammer Beetlejuice a run for his money in the skeeze department. This red meat steak tip recipe pays homage to Moseley's manic cannibal.

SERVINGS 4 • **PREP TIME** 15 MINUTES • **MARINATE TIME** 1-8 HOURS
COOK TIME 10 MINUTES

INGREDIENTS

STEAK TIPS
1½ lb sirloin steak
2 Tbsp olive oil

MARINADE
1 cup balsamic vinegar
½ cup extra-virgin olive oil
½ tsp dried rosemary
½ tsp dried oregano
2 cloves garlic, crushed
½ tsp kosher salt
½ tsp freshly ground black pepper

RED PEPPER CHIMICHURRI
⅓ cup olive oil
2 Tbsp red wine vinegar
½ cup jarred roasted red peppers
1 clove garlic
¼ tsp dried oregano
3 Tbsp chopped fresh parsley, plus more for garnish
½ tsp salt
¼ tsp freshly ground black pepper
¼ tsp crushed red pepper flakes

DIRECTIONS

❶ Cut the steak into pieces a little bigger than bite size. Place in a container with a cover. In a large jar, mix together all marinade ingredients, close and shake to combine. Pour marinade over steak, mix to coat evenly, cover and refrigerate for at least 1 hour or up to 8 hours.

❷ Remove the jar from the refrigerator, then remove steak from marinade. Dry the meat with a paper towel and let come to room temperature.

❸ Meanwhile, place all red pepper chimichurri ingredients into a blender and pulse until a small chunky consistency is achieved.

❹ In a large pan (cast iron works great in this recipe) with oil on medium-high heat, sear steak on all sides, cooking in batches to not overcrowd the pan.

❺ Place the beef onto a serving plate, drizzle with chimichurri and garnish with extra chopped parsley.

DISEMBODIED SPATCHCOCKED CHICKEN

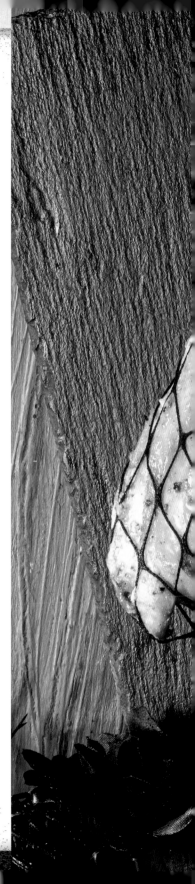

After his wedding scheme to living teenager Lydia Deetz falls through a giant sandworm-shaped hole in the ground, Beetlejuice finds himself in the waiting room of the Netherworld. Sitting next to a pair of legs (sans torso) in fishnets, true to maximum creep style, Beetlejuice tries to pull a move but is smacked hard by the owner of said legs—a magician's assistant whose last performance went awry. This spatchcocked chicken recipe, which you can carve into equal halves, gives a nod to the unfortunately disembodied magician's assistant in the waiting room—tempting legs and all.

SERVINGS 4 • **PREP TIME** 10 MINUTES • **COOK TIME** 40 MINUTES

INGREDIENTS

- 1 (1-5-lb) chicken
- ⅓ cup plain yogurt
- Zest and juice of 2 lemons
- ½ tsp paprika
- ½ tsp onion powder
- 2 cloves garlic, minced
- 1 tsp dried oregano
- ½ tsp salt
- ½ tsp freshly ground black pepper

DIRECTIONS

❶ Preheat the oven to 375 degrees F.

❷ Remove the backbone from the chicken with poultry shears. Crack the chicken open to lay flat.

❸ In a medium bowl, mix remaining ingredients.

❹ Place the chicken in a large baking dish and top with the yogurt mixture. Place in oven and cook for about 40 minutes or until the internal temperature reaches 165 degrees F. Let rest for 10 minutes before cutting.

EVERYTHING BUT THE KITCHEN SINK PASTA

Sometimes, you've got to work with what you've got. No one knows this better than Delia Deetz when brought face-to-face with the reality of her new home in Winter River. Charles similarly puts on a big show of encouraging his family to love their new home by leaning into a chipper, can-do attitude. Take, for example, the first time the family explores the kitchen and Charles realizes all the plumbing needs to be replaced. This recipe takes Charles's attitude to the max by working with several disparate but common pantry items that will have you whipping up an impressive pasta dinner with minimal cost, effort and stress.

SERVINGS 4–6 • **PREP TIME** 15 MINUTES • **COOK TIME** 12 MINUTES

INGREDIENTS

- 1 (12-oz) box cellentani pasta
- 1 (1-lb) chicken breast, cut into bite-size pieces
- 1 tsp cajun seasoning
- ¼ cup all-purpose flour
- 2 Tbsp olive oil
- 1 small yellow onion, diced
- 1 small orange pepper, diced
- 1 pint grape/cherry tomatoes
- 6 oz frozen broccoli
- 2 cloves garlic, minced
- 1 cup chicken broth
- 1 cup heavy cream
- ½ tsp salt
- ½ tsp freshly ground black pepper

DIRECTIONS

❶ Cook pasta according to package directions.

❷ Season the chicken with 1 tsp cajun seasoning, then coat with flour.

❸ In a large skillet with oil on medium-high heat, brown the chicken on all sides (cook in batches to not overcrowd the pan). Remove from pan and set aside.

❹ In the same pan, add more oil if needed, lower the heat to medium and cook the onion, pepper, half of the tomatoes and broccoli for 3 to 4 minutes, stirring often. Add the garlic and cook for another minute. Stir in the broth, cream, salt and pepper and bring to a simmer. Place the chicken back into the pan and cook for another 3 to 5 minutes or until cooked through. Stir in the pasta and add remaining cherry tomatoes on top.

I'M STUFFED BONE-IN CHICKEN BREAST

T he Maitlands turn to their *Handbook for the Recently Deceased*, mostly in frustration and as a last resort, and are shocked when the "In Case of Emergency" section instructions (draw a door, knock three times) actually work. Following the door into the Netherworld, the Maitlands find themselves in the afterlife's waiting room, surrounded by other dead folks. One such unfortunate soul is Ferndock, a man who apparently died choking on a chicken bone that is still protruding from his throat. This bone-in stuffed chicken breast is Ferndock approved—just be careful with the bones, lest you end up in the afterlife forevermore sporting a chicken bib.

SERVINGS 4 • **PREP TIME** 15 MINUTES • **COOK TIME** 10 MINUTES

INGREDIENTS

ORZO STUFFING
- 1 cup cooked orzo
- 1 Tbsp chopped fresh parsley
- 1 Tbsp chopped fresh shallot
- 4 oz baby spinach, chopped
- 2 Tbsp Parmesan cheese
- ¼ cup cream cheese, room temperature
- ¼ cup shredded mozzarella cheese

CHICKEN
- 4 chicken breasts with wing bone attached (chicken supreme)
- ½ tsp salt
- ¼ tsp freshly ground black pepper
- 1 tsp dried parsley
- 1 tsp dried basil
- ¼ tsp paprika
- ¼ tsp onion powder

WINE-CAPER SAUCE
- 3 Tbsp butter, divided
- 1 clove garlic, minced
- 2 Tbsp shallots, minced
- ¼ cup dry white wine
- ¾ cup chicken broth
- 2 Tbsp capers
- 1 tsp chopped fresh parsley
- ⅛ tsp salt
- ⅛ tsp freshly ground black pepper
- 2 Tbsp fresh lemon juice

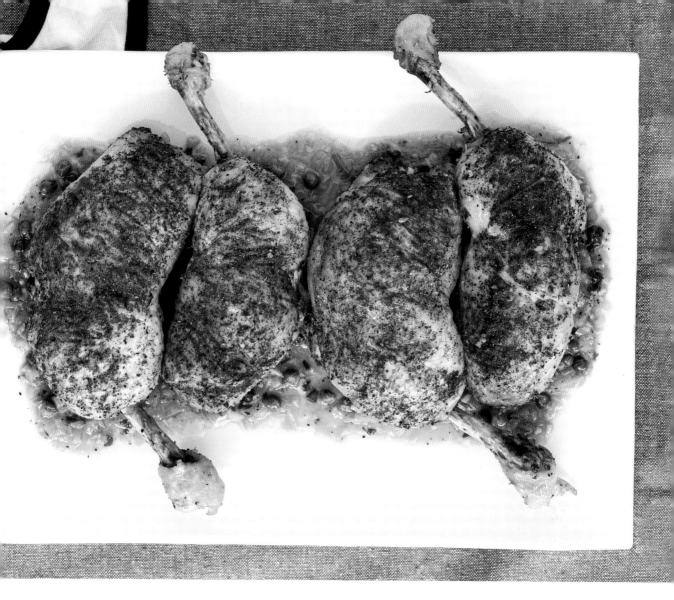

DIRECTIONS

❶ Mix all stuffing ingredients.

❷ Preheat the oven to 350 degrees F.

❸ Cut around the tip of the wing bone, right under the knob of the bone. Push the skin and meat down to expose the bone. Scrape the bone clean and wrap with foil. Cut a pocket into the chicken on the end without the wing bone. Stuff each pocket with an even amount of stuffing. Secure with a toothpick.

❹ In a small bowl, mix the salt, pepper, parsley, basil, paprika and onion powder. Season chicken evenly with the mixture. Place the chicken in a baking dish and cook for 30 to 40 minutes or until the internal temperature reaches 165 degrees F.

❺ Meanwhile, in a skillet with 2 Tbsp butter on medium-low heat, cook the garlic and shallots for 1 to 2 minutes, stirring often. Bring to medium heat, stir in the wine and cook for another 1 to 2 minutes. Stir in the broth, capers, parsley, salt and pepper. Simmer for 2 to 3 minutes to thicken. Remove from heat and stir in lemon juice and remaining butter.

❻ Place the sauce, then the chicken, on a serving plate.

IT'S ALL GOOD, BRO FISH TACOS

I n their time waiting for their caseworker Juno, the Maitlands get a full dose of different folks who find themselves stuck in eternity (see Disembodied Spatchcocked Chicken, pg. 56; I'm Stuffed Bone-In Chicken Breast, pg. 60). Another Netherworld waiting room inhabitant is a beach bro who appears to have had a totally radical encounter with a shark, which is still attached to his leg (probably forever, given the way this version of the afterlife works.). Death-by-shark is a rough way to go, but at least Beach Bro can take some solace in this recipe. Fish tacos won't heal a lethal shark bite, but they taste like heaven.

SERVINGS 4 • **PREP TIME** 12 MINUTES
COOK TIME 6 MINUTES

INGREDIENTS

SLAW
- 2 cups cole slaw mix
- ¼ cup mayonnaise
- ¼ tsp celery seeds
- ¼ cup chopped fresh cilantro
- 1 lime, juiced
- 1 Tbsp honey
- ¼ tsp salt
- ¼ tsp freshly ground black pepper

BEER-BATTERED FISH
- 1 cup all-purpose flour
- 1 tsp salt
- 1 egg, beaten
- ½ tsp baking powder
- 1⅓ cup Mexican beer
- ½ tsp hot sauce
- Oil for frying
- 1¼ lb halibut fish fillets, cut into 2-by-1-inch strips
- 12 fresh corn tortillas

TOPPINGS
- ⅓ cup crumbled queso blanco
- ½ red onion, thinly sliced
- 2 limes, cut into wedges

DIRECTIONS

❶ In a medium bowl, mix all slaw ingredients.

❷ In a large bowl, mix the flour, salt, egg, baking powder, beer and hot sauce.

❸ Fill a pan with 2 to 3 inches of oil and heat to 350 to 360 degrees F.

❹ In batches to avoid overcrowding, dip the fish pieces into the beer batter and cook in the hot oil for about 3 minutes or until golden brown. Drain on a wire rack.

❺ Microwave the tortillas folded in a damp paper towel for 20 to 30 seconds.

❻ Fill the tacos with an even amount of fried fish, then top with an even amount of slaw, queso blanco and red onion. Serve with limes.

KEATON'S AD-LIBBED TACO BAR

In addition to coming up with Beetlejuice's overall look, Michael Keaton also famously ad-libbed most of his lines for the film—including but not limited to BJ's rattled-off credentials upon first meeting the Maitlands (see (Un)holy Guacamole, pg. 24) and the scene in which he accidentally kicks over a prop tree while in the Winter River model. When cooking, as with acting, sometimes the magic comes from ad-libbing. This versatile taco bar can be modified any way you—the director and main character of your meal—want.

MAKES ABOUT 16 TACOS • **PREP TIME** 7–10 MINUTES
COOK TIME 6–10 MINUTES

SHELL OPTIONS

Tortillas
Hard shells
Bib lettuce

FILLINGS

CHICKEN
(use sliced portobellos for a vegetarian option)

- 1 tsp chili powder
- ½ tsp ground cumin
- ½ tsp garlic powder
- ½ tsp smoked paprika
- ¼ tsp cayenne pepper
- ½ tsp sugar
- ¼ tsp salt
- ¼ tsp freshly ground black pepper
- 2 lb chicken, cut into bite-size pieces
- 2 Tbsp olive oil

Mix all the spices together in a bowl. Coat chicken (or portobellos) with spice mix. In a large pan with oil on medium-high, cook chicken until browned on all sides and the internal temperature reaches 165 degrees F.

BEEF

- ¼ cup soy sauce
- ¼ cup lime juice
- 3 cloves garlic, minced
- 1 Tbsp cumin
- 1 Tbsp chili powder
- 1 tsp smoked paprika
- 1 tsp dried oregano
- 2 lb skirt steak

❶ Mix all ingredients except steak. Place the steak in a container and cover with the marinade for at least 1 hour or up to overnight. Dry the steak with a paper towel and bring to room temperature. ❷ Preheat the grill to medium-high heat. Grill

½ red onion, finely
    chopped
1 clove garlic, minced
½ jalapeño, seeded and
    diced
1 tsp chopped fresh
    cilantro
1 lime, juiced
¼ tsp cumin
½ tsp sugar
½ tsp salt
¼ tsp freshly ground black
    pepper

Mix all ingredients in a
bowl. Let sit for 1 hour or
pulse in a food processor if
desired.

SLAW
(See It's All Good, Bro Fish
Tacos, pg. 62)

AVOCADO CREMA
¼ cup sour cream or
    crema
1 avocado
1 lime, juiced
¼ tsp salt
¼ tsp freshly ground black
    pepper

Place all ingredients in a
blender and blend until
smooth.

ADD-ONS
Shredded cheddar
    cheese
Shredded lettuce

the steak about 4 to 5
minutes on each side or
until internal temperature
reaches 135 degrees F. Let
rest for 10 minutes, then
slice against the grain.

BEER-BATTERED FISH
(See It's All Good, Bro Fish
Tacos, pg. 62)

TOPPINGS
PICKLED ONIONS
1 large red onion, peeled
    and very thinly sliced
¼ cup apple cider vinegar
¼ cup distilled vinegar
¼ cup water
1 tsp peppercorns
1 tsp salt
1 Tbsp sugar

Place the sliced onions
in a mason jar. In a small
saucepan, bring the
remaining ingredients to a
boil. Pour the mixture into
the jar. Seal with the lid
and refrigerate to cool.

GUACAMOLE
(See (Un)holy Guacamole,
pg. 24)

SALSA
4 cups chopped fresh
    tomatoes

MAITLAND MEATLOAF

Attractive, unassuming and wholesome, Adam and Barbara Maitland are regular fixtures in Winter River, Connecticut—Adam owns and operates the local hardware store (Maitland Hardware), while Barb is constantly at work on the interior of their beautiful Victorian home. At the beginning of *Beetlejuice*, the couple is starting an exciting vacation: taking a week off of work, painting models to fit in Adam's replica of Winter River and re-wallpapering rooms. It follows that Barbara and Adam would enjoy this Americana-as-it-gets dish as a staple in the Maitland household. For maximum effect, serve with milk.

SERVINGS 6–8 • **PREP TIME** 10 MINUTES • **COOK TIME** 1 HOUR

INGREDIENTS

- 2 lb ground beef
- 1 small onion, finely chopped
- ½ green bell pepper, finely chopped
- ½ red bell pepper, finely chopped
- 2 large eggs, lightly beaten
- 2 cloves garlic, minced
- 1 Tbsp dried parsley
- ¾ cup seasoned breadcrumbs
- ¾ cup milk
- 1 Tbsp Worcestershire sauce
- ½ tsp salt
- ½ tsp freshly ground black pepper
- 1 Tbsp olive oil
- ¾ cup marinara sauce

DIRECTIONS

❶ Preheat the oven to 350 degrees F.

❷ In a large bowl, mix all ingredients except the oil and marinara.

❸ Grease a baking dish with olive oil. Add the meatloaf mixture and form into a loaf. Top with the sauce and cook for 50 to 60 minutes or until the internal temperature reaches 160 degrees F.

❹ Let rest for 5 minutes before slicing.

FANCY PANTS
LOBSTER
MAC AND CHEESE

In the film, Delia Deetz is seen single-handedly preparing a rather expansive dinner for seven guests, all of whom she is desperate to impress. With so many tasks to tackle, Delia doesn't appreciate Lydia's interjection that honest-to-goodness ghosts live in their house.

She dismisses her stepdaughter's photographic evidence with a wave of her chef's knife. Though we never get to see Delia's main course, this decadent mac and cheese dotted with tender chunks of lobster would absolutely earn a spot on her impeccably styled, 1988 cut stone dinner table.

SERVINGS 6 • **PREP TIME** 15 MINUTES • **COOK TIME** 40 MINUTES

INGREDIENTS

MAC AND CHEESE
- 16 oz 3-cheese tortellini
- 3 Tbsp butter
- 3 Tbsp all-purpose flour
- 3 cups whole milk
- ¼ tsp nutmeg
- ¼ tsp salt
- ¼ tsp pepper
- 2 cups shredded cheddar cheese
- 1 cup shredded Gruyère
- 1 lb cooked lobster, cut into bite-size pieces

CRUNCHY TOPPING
- 3 slices cooked bacon, crumbled
- ¼ cup seasoned breadcrumbs
- ¼ cup panko

DIRECTIONS

❶ Preheat the oven to 350 degrees F.

❷ In a large pot of boiling salted water, cook tortellini according to package directions.

❸ In a large saucepan, melt the butter on medium-low heat. Whisk in flour and cook for about 1 minute. Slowly whisk in the milk, then stir in the nutmeg, salt and pepper. Stir in the cheese and continue to cook until the cheese has melted and the sauce has thickened, stirring frequently. Add tortellini and lobster to the cheese sauce and mix to combine. Transfer mixture to a large baking dish.

❹ In a small bowl, mix together bacon, breadcrumbs and panko. Sprinkle the mixture over tortellini and place in the oven.

❺ Cook for 20 to 25 minutes or until the cheese is bubbly at the edges and the top is slightly browned.

MISS ARGENTINA FLANK STEAK

T he former beauty contestant who works reception in the afterlife's version of the DMV, Miss Argentina, is skeptical, opinionated and annoyed by newbie ghost nonsense. Casually rattling off stipulations under which a ghost can accrue D-90 help vouchers (it takes 125 years for three of them), Miss Argentina also drops the twist that had she known what she now knows when she was alive, she wouldn't have "accidentally" slit her wrists. This flank steak is best served with a heaping dose of Argentine-inspired salad—and bloody is better.

SERVINGS 4 • **PREP TIME** 15 MINUTES
COOK TIME 10 MINUTES

INGREDIENTS

TOMATO SALAD
- 3 ripe tomatoes, chopped into ½-inch pieces
- 1 serrano pepper, sliced
- 3 mini red peppers, sliced into rounds

DRESSING
- 3 Tbsp red wine vinegar
- ¼ cup olive oil
- 1 clove garlic, minced
- ¼ tsp paprika
- ¼ tsp dried oregano
- ½ tsp onion powder
- ½ tsp salt
- ⅛ tsp freshly ground black pepper
- ⅛ tsp parsley
- ⅛ tsp red pepper flakes

STEAK
- 2 lb flank steak
- ½ tsp salt
- ½ tsp freshly ground black pepper

DIRECTIONS

❶ In a medium bowl, mix the tomatoes, serrano pepper and red peppers.
❷ Place dressing ingredients in a jar, close lid and shake to mix. Pour the desired amount of dressing onto the tomato salad, then toss to coat.

❸ Preheat the grill to medium-high. Season the steak with salt and pepper and grill for 3 to 5 minutes on each side or until the internal temperature reaches 130 degrees F. Take the steak off the grill and let rest for 10 minutes.

❹ Slice the steak into thin slices against the grain. To serve, top with salad in a "slash" style.

NEITHERWORLD PICNIC SPREAD

T he 1980s and '90s were an interesting time in which hit films could see ongoing success as animated TV shows (see *Ghostbusters*, *The Mask* and *Bill and Ted's Excellent Adventure*). The *Beetlejuice* animated series gives the eponymous character more of a Disney's *Aladdin* Genie vibe, expanding the Netherworld (and also changing its name to Neitherworld) into a cool place that animated Lydia can visit with her BFF BJ. The series also relies on puns to fuel its slapstick humor—take for example an episode that inspired this recipe, in which Beetlejuice and Lydia are enjoying a picnic served with "maca-groany salad," "corn on the slob" and "strawberry snortcakes."

MACA-GROANY SALAD

SERVINGS 8–10 • **PREP TIME** 15 MINUTES • **COOK TIME** 10 MINUTES

INGREDIENTS

12 oz elbow macaroni	2 scallions, chopped
1 cup mayonnaise	1 carrot, shredded
1 Tbsp Dijon mustard	1 tsp dried parsley
1 stalk celery, diced	1 tsp Cajun seasoning
½ red bell pepper, diced	

DIRECTIONS

❶ In a large pot of salted boiling water, cook pasta according to package directions. Drain and let cool.

❷ In a large bowl, mix all remaining ingredients. Add pasta and stir to combine.

❸ Cover and place in the refrigerator to cool completely. Add more mayonnaise if needed.

CORN ON THE SLOB

SERVINGS 6 • **PREP TIME** 17 MINUTES • **COOK TIME** 10 MINUTES

INGREDIENTS

WHITE BARBECUE SAUCE
- ¾ cup mayonnaise
- ½ Tbsp cream-style horseradish
- 1 Tbsp apple cider vinegar
- ½ tsp yellow mustard
- ⅛ tsp salt
- ⅛ tsp freshly ground black pepper
- ⅛ tsp cayenne pepper

CORN
- 4 ears corn
- ½ cup store-bought barbecue sauce or see The Cal Worthington Special (pg. 86)

DIRECTIONS

❶ In a medium bowl, mix all sauce ingredients.
❷ Preheat the grill to medium heat.
❸ Brush the corn with store-bought barbecue sauce. Grill for about 10 minutes, turning to cook all sides until the sauce caramelizes, brushing more sauce on each turn.
❹ Remove from grill, place on a serving plate and drizzle with the white barbecue sauce.

STRAWBERRY SNORTCAKES

SERVINGS 6 • **PREP TIME** 15 MINUTES • **COOK TIME** 40 MINUTES

INGREDIENTS

- 10 oz fresh strawberries, halved
- ¾ cup sugar
- 1 box strawberry cake mix
- 4 cups whipped topping
- 1 cup crushed strawberry shortcake cookies
- 6 sprigs mint

DIRECTIONS

❶ Mix strawberries and sugar in a medium bowl. Set aside.
❷ Choose 6 jars for serving. Make the cake according to package directions. When the cake is cooled, cut into rounds that will fit inside the jars. Place a piece of cake on the bottom of each jar.
❸ Create even, repeating layers of whipped topping, strawberries and cookies in each jar. Garnish each with a sprig of mint.

ORANGE (JUICE) CHICKEN

The Deetz family isn't the easiest to identify with, especially when Barbara and Adam (and the audience) first encounter them. Delia's immediate urge is to tear things down and replace them with her unique artist's perspective. Charles gives off major yuppie-who-doesn't-know-anything-about-country-home-ownership (but will dress the part) vibes and Lydia initially seems sullen and standoffish. But the first night after moving in, the Deetzes start to become more relatable—a large part of that starts with their first dinner together around Chinese takeout. This juicy take on the popular chicken dish pairs well with a hefty serving of noodles (see It's Chowtime! Chow Mein, pg. 52) and will make a good impression on anyone you share it with.

SERVINGS 4 • **PREP TIME** 15 MINUTES • **COOK TIME** 20 MINUTES

INGREDIENTS

ORANGE SAUCE
- 1 (18-oz) jar orange marmalade
- ¼ cup orange juice
- 1 Tbsp soy sauce
- 1 Tbsp freshly grated ginger
- 1 clove garlic, minced
- ¼ tsp crushed red pepper

CHICKEN
- 1½ cups flour
- ¼ cup cornstarch
- ½ tsp salt
- ½ tsp freshly ground black pepper
- 2 eggs
- 2 lb chicken breasts, cut into bite-size pieces
- Oil for frying

GARNISH
- 2 green onions, sliced
- 1 Tbsp white sesame seeds

DIRECTIONS

❶ Heat the oil to 350–360 degrees F.

❷ In a small saucepan on medium heat, mix all orange sauce ingredients. Simmer for 5 minutes, stirring often. Set aside. If a smoother texture is desired, the sauce can be blended.

❸ In a shallow bowl, mix together the flour, cornstarch, salt and pepper. In another shallow bowl, beat the eggs together. Coat the chicken with the egg then dredge the chicken into the flour to coat.

❹ In batches to avoid overcrowding, cook the chicken in oil until golden brown and cooked through. Drain on a paper towel.

❺ Coat the chicken with orange sauce. Garnish with green onions and sesame seeds.

ORION'S
BETELGEUSE BURGER

Originally, *Beetlejuice* was conceived as a much scarier straight horror movie with a demonic character inspired by *The Exorcist*. This darker, earlier script reportedly had Beetlejuice emerge as a murdering winged demon who ends up slaughtering the Deetzes. After numerous rewrites, the movie became the off-kilter dark comedy we know and love, though certain elements from the original script still made their way into the final product, including the bio-exorcist's name. While the film's title was updated to a phonetic spelling, the Ghost With the Most keeps his original name (Betelgeuse), as seen in the commercials and flyers he posts to try to win the Maitlands' business. Betelgeuse, of course, is the 10th-brightest star in our night sky and the second-brightest in the constellation Orion. It also looks a bit like a runny egg and is believed by astronomers to be exploding—inspiring this delightful, not-demonic-at-all burger.

SERVINGS 4 • **PREP TIME** 10 MINUTES • **COOK TIME** 10 MINUTES

INGREDIENTS

- 1½ lb ground beef
- 1 Tbsp salt
- 1 Tbsp freshly ground black pepper
- 4 slices yellow American cheese
- 2 Tbsp butter
- 4 eggs
- ½ cup mayonnaise
- 4 brioche buns, toasted
- 4 large dark lettuce leaves
- 4 slices yellow artisanal tomato
- 4 slices cooked crisp bacon

DIRECTIONS

❶ Form 4 even burgers from the beef and season with salt and pepper. In a large cast iron pan, cook the burgers on medium-high heat for 3 minutes. Flip, cook for 2 more minutes, then top each with a slice of cheese. Cover the pan and continue to cook until the cheese has melted and the burger is medium.

❷ In a non-stick pan with butter on medium-low heat, cook the eggs for 1 to 2 minutes or until the whites are cooked enough to flip. Flip the eggs and continue to cook another minute or just until the whites are cooked and the yolks are still runny.

❸ Spread mayonnaise on bottom buns and follow with lettuce, tomato, a burger, bacon and a cooked egg.

PARTY LIKE A ROMAN
RACK OF LAMB

Betelgeuse—derived from the Arabic yad al-jauza—isn't the only name of ancient and non-English background used in *Beetlejuice*. Otho Fenlock, friend of the Deetzes and their hypeman/interior decorator with a fabulous personal wardrobe, was named for the infamous and short-lived Roman Emperor who killed himself after three months at the top. Juno, the Maitlands' chain-smoking, power suit and pearl-clad afterlife caseworker, was named for the Roman goddess of women, marriage and childbirth (known more broadly as the Greek goddess Hera). This take on rack of lamb celebrates Otho and Juno's Roman heritage—in Ancient Rome, lamb chops were a staple of large parties.

SERVINGS 4 • **PREP TIME** 10 MINUTES • **COOK TIME** 10 MINUTES

INGREDIENTS

CHERRY-MINT SAUCE
- 2 Tbsp butter
- 1 (10-oz jar) cherry spreadable fruit
- ½ tsp Dijon mustard
- 2 fresh mint leaves, minced
- 1 clove garlic, minced
- ⅛ tsp red pepper flakes
- ⅛ tsp salt
- ⅛ tsp freshly ground black pepper

LAMB
- 2 racks of lamb, Frenched (about 2 lb)
- ½ tsp salt
- ½ tsp freshly ground black pepper

DIRECTIONS

❶ In a small saucepan, add all sauce ingredients. On low heat, cook until the sauce has thickened slightly (about 3 to 5 minutes), stirring often. Remove from the heat and let come to room temperature.

❷ Preheat the oven to 400 degrees F.

❸ Place the ribs onto a baking sheet rib side down. Rub with salt and pepper, then brush with the sauce. Cook for 20 minutes or until the internal temperature reaches 135 degrees F. Remove and let the lamb rest tented with foil for 10 minutes before slicing.

SCARED SHEETLESS SHEET PAN FAJITAS

Beetlejuice hardly had a smooth road to getting filmed and released, and the same goes for the name of the main character (see Orion's Betelgeuse Burger, pg. 76) and the title of the film itself. Burton reportedly made a joke to the studio that the film should be called *Scared Sheetless*—which nearly became the final title until the director put his foot down to make *Beetlejuice* happen. This recipe proves sheet pan fajitas are not scary but instead simple and versatile no matter what you call them.

SERVINGS 4 • **PREP TIME** 12 MINUTES
COOK TIME 6 MINUTES

INGREDIENTS

- 2 lb boneless, skinless chicken breasts, cut into 1-by-1½-inch strips
- 4 mini red peppers, deseeded, sliced into rounds
- 4 mini yellow peppers, deseeded, sliced into rounds
- 2 chilaca peppers or any thin green or red pepper, deseeded
- 3 green bell peppers, deseeded and sliced
- 2 yellow onions, sliced
- 2 Tbsp olive oil
- 2 Tbsp fajita seasoning
- 2 cloves garlic, minced
- 8 (8-inch) flour tortillas
- 1 lime, cut into wedges
- 1 small bunch fresh cilantro, chopped

DIRECTIONS

❶ Preheat the oven to 425 degrees F.

❷ Place the chicken, peppers and onions onto the sheet pan. Drizzle with oil and season with the fajita seasoning, then toss to coat.

❸ Place the sheet pan in oven and cook for 10 minutes. Remove, add garlic, then continue to cook another 10 minutes or until the internal temperature of the chicken reaches 165 degrees F.

❹ Serve with tortillas, lime wedges and cilantro.

SESAME BROILED SALMON

Despite being banished from the high society of Manhattan to the middle of nowhere in Connecticut, Delia is determined to make her new environment work. Her first big test is hosting a memorable dinner party in her newly renovated house—and nothing, especially not her stepdaughter's rumored "ghosts" in the attic, will stop her. As with the other dishes on Delia's dinner party list (see Manhattan Hand Rolls, pg. 38; Showstopper Shrimp Cocktail, pg. 36; and Fancy Pants Lobster Mac and Cheese, pg. 68), this signature dish embraces 1980s seafood trends by leaning into Japanese-inspired flavors. Roasted salmon is always a crowd-pleaser, but bonus points are awarded for black and white sesame seeds to fully embrace the *Beetlejuice* aesthetic.

SERVINGS 4 • **PREP TIME** 7 MINUTES • **COOK TIME** 16 MINUTES

INGREDIENTS

- 2 cloves garlic, minced
- 2 Tbsp ketchup
- 1 tsp soy sauce
- 1 tsp mustard
- 1 tsp honey
- 1 tsp brown sugar
- 2 dashes hot sauce
- 4 (8-oz) salmon fillets
- 1 Tbsp white sesame seeds, optional
- 1 Tbsp black sesame seeds, optional

DIRECTIONS

❶ Combine garlic, ketchup, soy sauce, mustard, honey, brown sugar and hot sauce in a small saucepan and simmer for about 4 minutes (the sauce should be thick). Remove from heat. Let come to room temperature.

❷ Preheat the oven to 375 degrees F.

❸ Grease a parchment-lined sheet pan with olive oil. Place the salmon onto the sheet pan and brush the sauce over each fillet. Cook in oven for 6 minutes, brush with more sauce and continue to cook for another 6 minutes or until cooked through.

❹ Garnish with white and black sesame seeds, if desired.

JUNO'S SMOKED BRISKET

One of the Maitlands' key helpers in the Netherworld is Juno, their caseworker. A tough-as-nails old gal, Juno is a semi-helpful bureaucrat who grudgingly gives the newly deceased couple important advice about getting rid of the Deetzes. Portrayed by veteran actor Sylvia Sidney, one of the many things that makes Juno unforgettable is her husky smoker's voice—a feature made more prominent as Juno is always smoking cigarettes in her scenes. Then there's the self-inflicted gash across her throat (that smoke pours out of, naturally). Smoking is decidedly bad for your health, but this brisket is good for your soul.

SERVINGS 4 • **PREP TIME** 10 MINUTES • **COOK TIME** 6–8 HOURS

INGREDIENTS

- 1 Tbsp salt
- 2 Tbsp packed brown sugar
- ½ tsp black pepper
- ½ tsp smoked paprika
- ½ tsp onion powder
- ½ tsp garlic powder
- ½ tsp cayenne pepper
- 1 tsp mustard powder
- ½ tsp cumin
- ½ tsp thyme
- 1 Tbsp chili powder
- ½ tsp dried parsley
- 5 lb packer brisket

DIRECTIONS

❶ Using cherry wood or your favorite hardwood, bring a smoker to 250 degrees F.
❷ In a medium bowl, mix all seasoning ingredients. Dry the brisket with a paper towel, then generously season on all sides.
❸ Place the brisket in the smoker fat side up and smoke for 6 to 8 hours or until internal temperature reaches 195 degrees F. Let rest for 30 minutes before slicing.

SERVING SUGGESTION

Place sliced beef on a serving plate with a glass dome top and fill the dome with smoke from a handheld smoker gun.

THE CAL WORTHINGTON
SPECIAL

C ar salesman Cal Worthington was infamous and ubiquitous in West Coast television ads from the 1960s through the 1980s. Part of a running gag, "smiling Cal's" commercials frequently featured "his dog, Spot" (who would never actually be a dog, but instead an exotic animal such as a chimpanzee or a lion), as well as claims that Cal would buy you an all-you-can-eat dinner in exchange for potential business. Parodies of (and characters inspired by) Cal Worthington have made their way into films and television over the years—from Ted Danson's Hal Jackson in *Made In America* to Michael Keaton's Beetlejuice. This blue plate special is inspired by the late, great Cal and the barbecue platter he promised.

SERVINGS (CHICKEN) 4 **SERVINGS (RIBS)** 4–6 • **PREP TIME** 17 MINUTES • **COOK TIME** 3 HOURS (TOTAL)

INGREDIENTS

BARBECUE SAUCE
- ½ tsp garlic powder
- ½ tsp onion powder
- 3 Tbsp hot sauce
- 3 cups ketchup
- 3 Tbsp apple cider vinegar
- 2 Tbsp brown sugar
- 2 tsp Dijon mustard
- 1 tsp smoked paprika
- ½ tsp salt
- 2 Tbsp steak sauce
- ½ tsp freshly ground black pepper

CHICKEN
- 2 lb bone-in, skin-on chicken pieces
- 1 tsp salt
- 1 tsp freshly ground black pepper

RIBS
- 2 racks of pork ribs
- 1 tsp salt
- 1 tsp freshly ground black pepper

NOTE: If making both chicken and ribs, double the sauce ingredients.

DIRECTIONS

BARBECUE SAUCE
Place all ingredients into a saucepan, bring to a simmer and cook with lid on (to prevent splattering) for 5 minutes, stirring often. Remove from heat and set aside.

CHICKEN
❶ Preheat the grill to medium heat.
❷ Season the chicken with salt and pepper.
❸ On a greased, preheated grill, cook chicken for 10 minutes, turning to brown on all sides. Brush chicken with sauce and cook for another 7 to 10 minutes or until the sauce has caramelized on all sides and the internal temperature is 165 degrees F. Remove from the grill, tent with foil and let rest for 10 minutes.

RIBS
❶ Bring one side of the grill to 225 degrees F.
❷ Season ribs with salt and pepper, then place on the side of the grill the flame is not on. Cook the ribs, turning every 30 minutes, for 2½ hours or until tender.
❸ Brush the sauce onto the ribs and cook on flame side of grill about 2 minutes on each side to caramelize the sauce.

TILL DEATH DO US PART
SPAGHETTI AND MEATBALLS

The opposite of power couple Charles and Delia Deetz, the wholesome Adam and Barbara Maitland are more interested in creating replica models, collecting toy horses and being homebodies. It's a good thing they happen to love each other and their house so much, as the couple gets stuck in that house together for eternity. Narrowly avoiding a botched séance turned exorcism, Barb and Adam find themselves clad in their wedding clothes the first time Charles and Delia are able to truly see them. Inspired by the Maitlands' steadfast devotion to each other—even after the "till death do us part" part—this classic pairing of spaghetti and meatballs is a dish you'll happily eat again and again and again. Just don't get any on your wedding garb.

SERVINGS 4–6 • **PREP TIME** 20 MINUTES • **COOK TIME** 40 MINUTES

INGREDIENTS

SAUCE
- 1 (32-oz) jar high-quality marinara sauce (e.g., Rao's)
- ¼ cup fresh basil leaves

MEATBALLS
- 2 Tbsp olive oil
- 1 small yellow onion, diced
- 2 cloves garlic, minced
- 1½ lb ground beef
- ½ cup seasoned breadcrumbs
- 2 slices white bread, crust removed, broken into very small pieces
- 2 Tbsp chopped fresh basil
- 1 Tbsp chopped fresh parsley
- ¼ cup grated Pecorino Romano cheese, plus more for serving
- ½ tsp salt
- ½ tsp freshly ground black pepper
- 2 eggs
- ⅓ cup milk

PASTA
- 2 Tbsp salt
- 1 lb spaghetti

DIRECTIONS

❶ In a heavy bottom pot, add the marinara sauce, basil and a half cup of water. Simmer, stirring often.

❷ In a small frying pan with olive oil on medium-low heat, cook the onions for about 2 minutes, then add in the garlic and cook for another minute. Remove from the heat and let cool.

❸ In a large bowl, add the remaining meatball ingredients, pouring the milk over the bread and breadcrumbs to moisten the bread. Add the onions and garlic. Mix to combine, but do not overmix. The mixture should be moist: Add more milk if needed. Form the meatballs a little bigger than golf balls.

❹ In a large frying pan on medium-high heat with enough oil to reach halfway up the meatballs, cook the meatballs in batches until browned on both sides.

❺ Place the cooked meatballs in the sauce. Skim some of the brown bits from the meatballs into the sauce. Continue to simmer, adding more water if needed. Skim off and discard the orange foam from the top of the sauce while it cooks. Simmer for another 20 minutes. Season with salt and pepper if needed.

❻ In a large pot of salted boiling water, cook the spaghetti according to package directions.

❼ Place some sauce into a serving bowl and top with the cooked pasta. Add more sauce and mix to coat. Place the meatballs on top and serve with extra sauce on the side and grated Pecorino Romano if desired.

Green and Purple
Meringues, pg. 98.

SNACKS

92 Tally Me Banana Bread

94 Freaky Fortune Cookies

96 Graveyard Dirt Pudding Cups

98 Green and Purple Meringues

100 In-Flight Roasted Nuts

102 Lost Souls Pretzel Ghosts

104 Scary Face Charcuterie

106 The Stray Dog

108 Troop 666 Girl Scout Cookies

TALLY ME
BANANA BREAD

Calypso music figures prominently in the *Beetlejuice* score. Even the opening credits with the first tinkling notes of Danny Elfman's main title sequence samples an eerie rendition of Harry Belafonte's "Banana Boat (Day-O)." Throughout the film, other Belafonte tracks feature as background noise but come into the foreground when the Maitlands try to regain control of their home from the Deetz family—most prominently, of course, for the dinner party scene. Why does calypso music feature so prominently in a zany, darkly comedic reverse haunted house movie set in small-town Connecticut? Why not? This recipe, incorporating Jamaican rum and bananas in a moist bread, should sate even the saltiest of new homeowners.

SERVINGS 8–10 • **PREP TIME** 10 MINUTES • **COOK TIME** 1 HOUR

INGREDIENTS

BANANA BREAD
- 2 cups flour, plus extra for pan
- ½ tsp baking soda
- 1 tsp baking powder
- ¾ cup brown sugar
- 1 tsp cinnamon
- 1 egg
- ¼ cup Jamaican rum
- ¼ cup melted butter
- ¾ cup milk
- 4 overripe bananas, 3 mashed

GLAZE
- 2 cups powdered sugar
- ¼ cup Jamaican rum

DIRECTIONS

❶ Preheat the oven to 350 degrees F.

❷ Spray an 8-by-4-inch loaf pan with cooking spray and dust with flour, shaking out excess flour.

❸ In a large bowl, mix the flour, baking soda, baking powder, sugar and cinnamon.

❹ Add in the egg, rum, melted butter, milk and 3 mashed bananas. Mix until just combined; do not overmix.

❺ Pour mix into pan. Cut the last banana in half lengthwise and place each half on top of the bread, pushing into the batter slightly. Bake for 50 to 60 minutes or until an inserted toothpick comes out clean. Remove and let cool for 10 minutes. Remove from pan and continue to cool on a wire rack.

❻ Mix the glaze ingredients and drizzle over bread.

FREAKY
FORTUNE COOKIES

It's a universal truth that after completing the ritual of moving, another important ritual must be observed: the devouring of takeout food. After the Deetz family manages to squeeze all of their impressive furniture, singular sculptures and other assorted belongings into their new Winter River home, they sit around containers of Chinese food [see It's Chowtime! Chow Mein (pg. 52) and Orange (Juice) Chicken (pg. 74)] and argue. One of the best parts of Chinese takeout is the fortune cookies. And in a haunted house, it's likely those cookies will foretell doom. For maximum effect when dreaming up appropriately grim fortunes, channel your inner ghoul.

MAKES 25–30 COOKIES • **PREP TIME** 20 MINUTES • **COOK TIME** 30 MINUTES

INGREDIENTS

- 3 large egg whites
- ¾ cup sugar
- ¼ cup water
- ½ tsp vanilla extract
- ¼ tsp almond extract
- 1 cup all-purpose flour
- 25 to 30 strips of paper, cut about .5" x 3" inches

DIRECTIONS

❶ Preheat the oven to 375 degrees F.

❷ Type or write foreboding fortunes, such as:
"Don't leave the house today."
"You will buy a home, and it is already haunted."
"The large crack will make the building fall."
"Your destiny is like a weakly sputtering flame."

❸ Line a sheet pan with parchment paper.

❹ In a mixer bowl with whisk attachment, whip egg whites until soft peaks form, then slowly add sugar. Whisk on high until hard peaks form and add in water, vanilla and almond extracts and flour until just combined.

❺ Working with a few cookies at a time, place 3-inch-thick circles of batter onto the lined baking sheet. Place in the oven and cook for 4 to 6 minutes or until the cookies are lightly browned.

❻ Take out of the oven and immediately add fortunes. Using a spatula, fold the circles in half, then fold ends of the cookie together by folding over the edge of a cup. Place each in a cupcake cup to hold its shape while cooling.

❼ Continue in the same manner, using all the batter.

Don't leave the house today

You will buy a home,
And it is already haunted

GRAVEYARD DIRT PUDDING CUPS

In the grand scheme of small-town life, Adam Maitland has a pretty sweet gig. A lovely wife, a beautiful house, a thriving hardware business—Adam's living the dream. His crowning achievement, the piece de resistance of his kingdom, is the scale model of Winter River that he keeps in the attic. Consistently working on adding to his model (at the beginning of the film, he's jazzed about the opportunity to use his vacation for model work), Adam's meticulous attention to detail wows even the jaded Deetzes when they finally see the model in the locked attic. This sweet snack is inspired by Adam's Winter River graveyard—just be sure to add your own flourishes to really make the model your own.

SERVINGS 12 • **PREP TIME** 12 MINUTES • **REFRIGERATOR TIME** 20 MINUTES

INGREDIENTS
- 1 (5.1-oz) box instant chocolate pudding
- 2 cups milk
- 2 (16-oz) containers whipped topping
- 24 Oreos

DIRECTIONS
❶ In a medium bowl, whisk together pudding mix and milk. Fold in half the whipped topping and refrigerate 10 minutes to set.
❷ Place the cookies in a food processor and pulse into a fine crumb.
❸ Layer the pudding and the remaining whipped topping into serving cups in a striped pattern. Top each with cookie crumbs. Refrigerate for 20 minutes before serving.

GREEN AND PURPLE MERINGUES

Cinematically, *Beetlejuice* is a tricky movie, employing challenging colors and imagery. The film's cinematographer, Thomas E. Ackerman, would later state that the film kept him on his toes stylistically and presented a refreshing challenge. Ackerman's visuals leaned into uncomfortable puke greens and industrial purples, especially vivid in the Netherworld. These color-swirled meringues share Ackerman's color palette—don't be afraid to experiment with the color swirl! Like with the film, even if things don't go quite to plan with this recipe, improvisation often pays off big time.

MAKES 45–55 MERINGUES • **PREP TIME** 20 MINUTES • **COOK TIME** 2 HOURS

INGREDIENTS

- 5 egg whites, room temperature
- 1 Tbsp vanilla
- ½ tsp cream of tartar
- 1 cup sugar
- 8–10 drops green food coloring
- 8–10 drops purple food coloring

DIRECTIONS

❶ Preheat the oven to 225 degrees F.

❷ Line 2 sheet pans with parchment paper.

❸ Using a mixer with a whisk attachment, whip the egg whites, vanilla and cream of tartar into soft peaks. Slowly add in the sugar, whisking on medium speed. On high speed, whip until hard peaks form (about 2 minutes).

❹ Place half of the meringue in a different bowl. Fold the green food coloring into one bowl and purple into the other. Place the green and purple meringue side by side onto a piece of plastic wrap. Roll the meringue up in the plastic, leaving one end open. Place the open side into a piping bag with a large piping tip.

❺ Pipe the meringue in rounds onto the sheet pans, spacing 1 inch apart. Cook for 30 minutes, turn pans and continue to cook for another 30 minutes. Turn off the oven and let the meringues sit in the oven for 1 hour or until set. Times may differ depending on humidity.

IN-FLIGHT ROASTED NUTS

One of the many interesting things about *Beetlejuice* is the number of Easter eggs throughout the film. When the Maitlands make their way to the Netherworld, a voice is heard over the PA system announcing the arrival of Flight 409. This is a reference to an actual flight that crashed in Wyoming in October 1955, killing all of the passengers aboard (the cause of the accident remains a mystery to this day). These roasted nuts are a savory, salty snack that shouldn't just be eaten in flight.

SERVINGS 2-4 • **PREP TIME** 5 MINUTES
COOK TIME 5 MINUTES

INGREDIENTS

- 4 Tbsp brown sugar
- 1 tsp ground cinnamon
- ½ tsp salt
- ¼ tsp cayenne pepper
- ½ tsp vanilla extract
- 2 Tbsp water
- 2 cups pecan halves

DIRECTIONS

❶ Mix all the ingredients except the pecans in a large non-stick pan. Cook on medium-high until the mixture is bubbly and thickened, stirring continuously. Stir in the pecans and mix to coat.

❷ Place the nuts on a baking sheet lined with parchment paper to cool. Once cooled, break the pecans apart.

LOST SOULS PRETZEL GHOSTS

On their first trip to the Netherworld, Adam and Barbara Maitland get quite a tour of the afterlife's bureaucracy. They also get a literal tour of the institution, learning that there's a fate worse than death—in fact, there can be death for the dead. The Lost Souls Room contains the tormented ghosts of those who have been exorcised. These adorable pretzels dipped in white chocolate with googly eyes are a cuter, tastier interpretation of those ghosts. Alternatively, if you prefer death and destruction, you can pretend to be a giant sandworm feasting on the poor unfortunate souls. Dealer's choice.

MAKES 12 PRETZEL GHOSTS • **PREP TIME** 10 MINUTES
COOK TIME 4 MINUTES

INGREDIENTS
12   oz white chocolate
15   pretzel rods
30   candy eyes

DIRECTIONS
❶ In a double boiler, melt the chocolate.
❷ Place pretzels on a large sheet of parchment paper. Carefully make ghost shapes by pouring the melted chocolate on top of the upper part of each pretzel (the bottom of the pretzel will be the handle). If desired, you can use a ghost stencil under the parchment. Place 2 candy eyes onto each and let cool.

SCARY FACE CHARCUTERIE

Beetlejuice's Scary Face, that is, the one revealed to the Maitlands but not to the audience, is a topic of interesting debate among fans of the film. The audience gets to see some hints at the face—creepy crawly things popping out of the side of his head—but very little else, other than Barbara and Adam's terrified reaction. The true face is left up to the audience's imagination, but luckily, you can put that imagination into practice with this charcuterie board that'll make your guests squeal (with delight).

SERVINGS 8–10 • **PREP TIME** 20 MINUTES • **COOK TIME** 5 MINUTES

INGREDIENTS

- 12 mini twist pretzels
- 5 oz dark chocolate
- 24 candy eyes
- 1 Styrofoam head
- ½ lb prosciutto
- ½ cup green olives
- ¼ cup In-Flight Roasted Nuts (pg. 100)
- 8 oz bite-size cubed pepper jack cheese
- 8 oz bite-size cubed pepperoni
- 8 oz brie cheese round
- ¼ cup raspberry jam
- ½ cup finger grapes, if available (or any grapes)
- ½ cup blackberries
- ½ cup black olives
- 6 oz sliced salami
  A variety of crackers, for serving

DIRECTIONS

❶ Make chocolate ghosts: In a double boiler, melt the chocolate. Dip the top 2 holes of the pretzels in the melted chocolate, leaving the bottom hole out. Place on a work surface lined with parchment paper. Place the candy eyes onto the top 2 holes. Set aside to harden.

❷ Place the Styrofoam head onto a serving platter and drape with prosciutto until covered. With toothpicks, place 2 green olives for each eye and secure In-Flight Roasted Nuts for teeth. Place the remaining olives and nuts on the serving platter.

❸ Place the cheese and pepperoni cubes onto wooden skewers. Insert the skewers into the Styrofoam head. Place any remaining ingredients on the platter.

❹ Place the brie on the platter, place a splat of raspberry jam on top (to resemble blood) and insert a cheese knife into the cheese. Serve the remaining jam in a small bowl.

❺ Skewer the grapes, blackberries and black olives individually onto skewers. Insert the skewers into the Styrofoam head. Arrange the remaining ingredients on the platter.

❻ Place the sliced salami onto skewers in a ribbon fashion and insert them into the Styrofoam head. Arrange the remaining salami on the serving platter.

❼ Place the chocolate ghosts on the platter.

❽ Serve with a variety of crackers.

THE STRAY DOG

Sometimes, the cause of one's demise is impossibly innocent and trivial. Enter the dog in *Beetlejuice*—a shaggy, sweet-looking pup (apparently named Rocket, according to an early script). This pooch is the sole reason the Maitlands find their home overtaken by Manhattanite interlopers and the target of a bio-exorcist con artist. Rocket causes the Maitlands to veer off the Winter River bridge. And then, while their Volvo dangles precariously at the end of a single beam, counterbalanced by the dog, what does said dog do? It trots away, leaving the Maitlands to plunge to their watery grave. These oh-so-good human treats (which are definitely not safe for dogs!) are inspired by this not-so-good boy.

MAKES 12 BREADSTICKS • **PREP TIME** 5 MINUTES
COOK TIME 20 MINUTES

INGREDIENTS

- 1 piece store-bought pizza dough
- 2 Tbsp butter, melted
- ¼ cup shredded cheddar cheese
- 2 Tbsp grated Parmesan cheese
- 2 cloves garlic, minced
- ¼ tsp freshly ground black pepper
- ½ tsp salt
- ½ tsp dried parsley

DIRECTIONS

❶ Preheat the oven to 350 degrees F.

❷ Roll out dough. Using a dog bone-shaped cookie cutter or a knife, cut 12 bones and place on a parchment paper-lined baking sheet.

❸ Brush the bones with butter. Top each with an even amount of the remaining ingredients.

❹ Bake for 15 to 20 minutes.

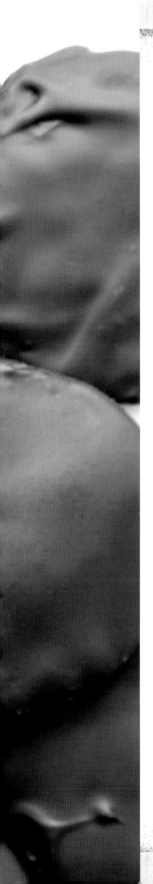

TROOP 666
GIRL SCOUT COOKIES

The Broadway adaptation of *Beetlejuice* takes some liberties with the source material, but it still stays true to the general storyline and aesthetic. The second act opens with an earnest Girl Scout named Sky who shares that because she has arrhythmia, a big scare might stop her heart. Though her parents have been very protective in the past, Sky is delighted to now be a Girl Scout selling cookies for the first time. She then visits the Deetz house...where she's scared by Beetlejuice. These cookies are in memory of Sky and her newfound fear of creepy old houses and ghouls in striped suits.

MAKES 36 COOKIES • **PREP TIME** 30 MINUTES • **COOK TIME** 11 MINUTES

INGREDIENTS

COOKIES
- 1½ cups flour
- ¾ cup unsweetened cocoa powder
- 1 tsp baking powder
- ¼ tsp salt
- ¾ cup unsalted butter, room temperature
- ¾ cup sugar
- 1 egg, room temperature
- 1 tsp pure vanilla extract
- ¼ tsp pure peppermint extract

CHOCOLATE
- 14 oz dark chocolate, chopped
- ¼ tsp vegetable oil
- ¼ tsp pure peppermint extract

DIRECTIONS

❶ In a medium bowl, mix flour, cocoa powder, baking powder and salt.

❷ In a mixer bowl with paddle attachment, cream the butter and sugar until pale and fluffy. Mix in the egg and both extracts. Slowly add in the dry ingredients until just combined; do not overmix.

❸ On a piece of parchment paper, roll the dough out about half a centimeter thick. Place the parchment paper with the dough on a baking sheet and freeze for 15 minutes.

❹ Preheat the oven to 350 degrees F.

❺ Remove dough from freezer and cut into 2-inch rounds with a cookie cutter.

❻ Bake for 9 to 11 minutes. Remove to a wire cooling rack.

❼ Melt the chocolate in a double broiler, then mix in the oil and peppermint. Dip each cookie into the chocolate, shaking off excess. Place on a piece of parchment paper to cool.

Supernatural
Sangria, pg. 118.

DRINKS

112 Coachless Spiked Punch

114 It's Vacation, Baby

116 Married in Red, Better off Dead
Bloody Mary

118 Supernatural Sangria

120 The Afterlife

122 Shrunken Head Cider

124 Spirit Lifter

126 Strange & Unusual

128 The Editor's Lunch

130 The Freelancer

132 The Jar

134 The Netherworld Bureaucrat

136 The Prince Valium

138 The Warning

140 Watery Grave

142 Gin & Juice! Gin & Juice!
Gin & Juice!

COACHLESS SPIKED PUNCH

While Barbara and Adam don't really "get" the afterlife and the very bizarre situation they find themselves in with the Deetz family, they do seem to understand the chain of authority. So, when the dead couple is forcibly summoned to the Netherworld by their caseworker, they comply, only to find Juno surrounded by a bunch of high school football players who didn't survive a plane crash. It turns out that while the team didn't make it out alive, their coach did—which is great for the coach, but not so great for the wayward football jocks, who are looking for a new authority figure to help them out (Juno doesn't seem particularly thrilled with this role, or with the Maitlands). This concoction is classic high school homecoming: you know, punch...unsupervised teenagers...liquor.

SERVINGS 24 • **PREP TIME** 5 MINUTES

INGREDIENTS

- 1 (28-oz) bottle Berry Blue Typhoon Hawaiian Punch
- 1 (2-L) bottle lemon-lime soda
- 8 oz blue Curaçao
- 12 oz vodka
- 12 oz rum
- 12 oz tequila
- 1 (8-oz) bag airplane gummies, optional

DIRECTIONS

Fill a punch bowl with ice. Add in the punch, soda and alcohol and mix. Top with gummies if desired.

IT'S VACATION, BABY

At the very beginning of *Beetlejuice*, the Maitlands exchange gifts to celebrate the start of a staycation in their fabulous old house in Winter River. Adam playfully pokes at Barbara because she's been up since 5 a.m. baking an American flag cake ("50 stars, 13 stripes—did you get it right this year?"). Barbara takes the teasing with a cheerful attitude—it's vacation! Vacations are also great for cocktails, as there are no responsibilities—just plenty of time for Maitland hobbies like adding to the model of Winter River and plastering more questionable wallpaper on the walls. This drink pairs well with either adorably dorky activity.

SERVINGS 4 • **PREP TIME** 7 MINUTES

INGREDIENTS

- 8 oz pineapple rum
- 8 oz banana rum
- 8 oz pineapple juice
- 8 oz cranberry juice
- 3 oz fresh lime juice
- 2 oz grenadine

GARNISH

- 4 maraschino cherries
- 4 fresh pineapple wedges
- 4 drink umbrellas

DIRECTIONS

❶ Mix the rums, juices and grenadine in a large pitcher.

❷ Fill 4 iced tea glasses with ice and pour an even amount of the mixture into each.

❸ Skewer a cherry and pineapple wedge. Garnish each glass with a skewer and a drink umbrella.

MARRIED IN RED, BETTER OFF DEAD BLOODY MARY

Beetlejuice is an interesting guy. He spends the entirety of the film trying to con the Maitlands with the ultimate goal of getting out of the ties that bind him to the afterlife. His ticket to freedom comes in the form of Lydia Deetz—he just needs to marry her in order to get out. In the interrupted wedding scene, Beetlejuice fashions Lydia in an unconventional (and if we're being honest, totally fabulous) red wedding dress. Of course, wearing red to a wedding hearkens to the old adage "married in red, better off dead"—a tongue-in-cheek symbolic choice in the film. This cocktail is a nod to Lydia's wedding attire—and really, there's nothing better than a bold-flavored Bloody Mary to take the edge off before being yanked down the aisle.

SERVINGS 4 • **PREP TIME** 12 MINUTES

INGREDIENTS

- 32 oz tomato juice
- 8 oz tequila
- ½ tsp celery seed
- 1 tsp Worcestershire sauce
- 5 dashes hot sauce
- 2 Tbsp prepared horseradish sauce
- ¼ tsp salt
- 1 tsp freshly ground black pepper
- ½ tsp paprika
- 1 Tbsp fresh lime juice

GARNISH

- 2 Tbsp Old Bay seasoning
- 4 lime wedges
- 8 pitted black olives
- 4 stalks celery
- 4 slices cooked crisp bacon
- 4 snow crab leg clusters

DIRECTIONS

❶ In a large pitcher, mix all Bloody Mary ingredients.

❷ Place the Old Bay seasoning onto a small round plate. Cut slits into the lime wedges, place onto the edge of 4 large glasses and rub around to wet the edges. Remove limes. Dip the rims into Old Bay to coat.

❸ Add ice to each glass and return limes to rims. Evenly fill each glass with the Bloody Mary mixture. Place 2 black olives onto 4 small skewers to fit onto the rim of the glass sideways. Place a celery stalk, a slice of bacon and a crab leg cluster into each glass.

SUPERNATURAL
SANGRIA

A s a feature film, *Beetlejuice* took an unconventional path to being written, getting greenlit, securing a director and talent and ultimately getting made. Originally envisioned as a dark, grizzly horror film, it took a few rewrites and Tim Burton at the helm to re-envision and reposition the film as the delightfully macabre comedy that ultimately made the cut. Now, *Beetlejuice* is a cult classic (if you're reading this cookbook, you probably already know that)—in fact, it's such a popular film that, on its 25th anniversary, Netflix shared that the very first DVD it shipped was *Beetlejuice* on March 10, 1998. So, if you're in the mood to Netflix and chill, this sublime sub-zero sangria recipe ought to hit the spot.

SERVINGS 10–12 • **PREP TIME** 10 MINUTES

INGREDIENTS

- 1 apple, cored and sliced
- 1 orange, sliced
- 1 cup sliced strawberries
- 1 cup blackberries
- 2 sticks cinnamon
- 1 (1½-L) bottle red wine
- 16 oz ginger ale
- 1 (25-oz) bottle semi-dry champagne

DIRECTIONS

In a large punch bowl, mix all the ingredients and add the ice.

THE AFTERLIFE

After the party, there's the after-party. And if you're one of the recently deceased, the party literally does not stop (especially if, like the Maitlands and the Deetzes, you're on Beetlejuice's hit list). This beet-forward hangover cure is guaranteed to make the morning after drinking with the Ghost with the Most at Dante's Inferno (see Dante's Inferno Hot Wings, pg. 28) feel a little less like the aftermath of an exorcism (see (Un) Holy Guacamole, pg. 24). Of course, if you've been partying with BJ, you may find it prudent to down a little hair of the dog by slipping some tequila into your fresh juice.

SERVINGS 4 • **PREP TIME** 5 MINUTES • **COOL TIME** 1 HOUR

INGREDIENTS
- 24 oz fresh beet juice
- 4 Tbsp fresh lemon juice
- 1 Tbsp grated fresh ginger
- 2 oranges
- 5 sprigs thyme, divided
  Tequila, optional

DIRECTIONS
❶ In a large pitcher, mix the beet juice, lemon juice, ginger, juice and zest from 1 orange and 1 thyme sprig. Refrigerate to cool and meld flavors for 1 hour.

❷ Slice the remaining orange into wedges. Place ice into 4 glasses. Pour an even amount into each glass (add 1 oz of tequila if desired) and garnish each with a sprig of thyme and an orange wedge on the rim.

SHRUNKEN HEAD CIDER

The waiting room in the afterlife is full of interesting characters—from the unfortunate magician's assistant (see Disembodied Spatchcocked Chicken, pg. 56) to the shark attack victim with the culprit still attached (see It's All Good, Bro Fish Tacos, pg. 62). Another memorable inhabitant is a hunter with a shrunken head, affectionately known as Harry the Hunter or I.M.

Smallhead to fans. Harry the Hunter presumably died due to a head shrinking performed by the man sitting next to him—a tribal doctor, who also gets some revenge by shrinking Beetlejuice's head in the film's last scene. This recipe calls for apple cider, complete with peeled and carved apples in the shape of shrunken heads—a "nod," if you will, to Harry the Hunter.

SERVINGS 8 • **PREP TIME** 15 MINUTES • **COOK TIME** 1 HOUR

INGREDIENTS

- 64 oz apple cider
- 1 orange, sliced
- ⅛ tsp nutmeg
- 3 cinnamon sticks
- 2 star anise pods
- 1 Tbsp whole cloves

GARNISH

- 8 carved apple skulls

DIRECTIONS

❶ Place the cider, orange slices, nutmeg, cinnamon, star anise and cloves into a slow cooker on high. Cook for 1 hour.

❷ Peel the apples with a paring knife. Carve the apples to look like skulls.

❸ Place skulls into 8 pint glasses and pour an even amount of cider into each glass.

SPIRIT LIFTER

G iven the fact that there's an afterlife in the *Beetlejuice* universe, one could make the leap to thinking there's really nothing to be scared of in death. Right? Wrong. When Barb and Adam take their inaugural tour of the Netherworld, they pass by the Lost Souls room (see Lost Souls Pretzel Ghosts, pg. 102) and learn that there actually is a fate worse than death for the undead. But while exorcism can be a real drag, this boozy concoction—a take on the classic reviver—is enough to elevate even the grimmest of spirits.

SERVINGS 1 • **PREP TIME** 5 MINUTES

INGREDIENTS

- 1 lime, zested then juiced
- 1 lime, cut into wedges
- 2 Tbsp coconut flakes
- 2 oz rumchata
- 2 oz white tequila
- ½ Tbsp triple sec

GARNISH
Dry ice, optional

DIRECTIONS

❶ Place the zest and coconut flakes onto a small plate. Cut slits into the lime wedges and run around the rims of a margarita glass. Dip rim into the coconut-lime mixture to coat.

❷ Fill the glass with ice.

❸ In a large cocktail shaker, add regular ice, rumchata, tequila, triple sec and 2 ounces lime juice from the zested lime. Shake to mix for 30 seconds. Pour into glass.

❹ Place a small piece of dry ice into glass, if desired. Note: Never touch dry ice. Let it melt before drinking.

STRANGE & UNUSUAL

When the Maitlands decide to turn to some old-school tricks to try and frighten the Deetz family from their home, they don't count on one member of the Deetz clan being able to see them. After snapping several Polaroids of the Maitlands' admittedly lackluster ghosts-in-sheets attempt, Lydia realizes that the duo wailing and wandering around the house are not her dad and stepmom (see No Feet Cloud Eggs, pg. 12). Barb and Adam are flabbergasted as to how she can possibly see them, even without the sheets. With classic deadpan delivery of arguably the best line in the entire film, Lydia pronounces that she can see the strange and unusual because she herself is strange and unusual. This drink is an ode to the lonely, impressively self-aware Deetz daughter.

SERVINGS 1 • **PREP TIME** 4 MINUTES

INGREDIENTS

- 2 oz black spiced rum
- 1 oz rumchata
- 4 oz ginger beer

DIRECTIONS

❶ Place the rum and rumchata into a large cocktail shaker with ice. Shake for 60 seconds.

❷ Pour into a champagne flute. Slowly add ginger beer and stir gently.

THE EDITOR'S LUNCH

D elia Deetz's infamous dinner party in her newly remodeled house boasts four guests, plus Charles, Lydia and Delia at the dining table. One of the guests happens to be a book editor for Ballantine Books, the sophisticated and slightly snooty Beryl, who apparently has a rather contentious relationship with Deetz family yes-man, Otho Fenlock. As an old-school book editor, Beryl gives major martini vibes—this drink, an homage to the old American classic three-martini lunch, fits his persona.

SERVINGS 1 • **PREP TIME** 5 MINUTES

INGREDIENTS

- 4 oz gin
- 1 oz dry vermouth
- 1 oz olive brine

GARNISH

- 3 olives

DIRECTIONS

❶ Chill martini glass in the freezer.

❷ In a large cocktail shaker, add ice, gin, vermouth and olive brine. Shake for 60 seconds.

❸ Pour into glass. Garnish with 3 skewered olives.

THE FREELANCER

Otho Fenlock is a truly underrated character. Possessing a sharp sense of personal fashion and an avant-garde eye for decoration, Otho positions himself as a freelance interior designer and Delia Deetz's on-call hype-man (as well as her shockingly dependable BFF). He's also full of surprises—throughout the film, Otho mentions that he was a hair analyst, and schooled in chemistry. Also, he used to be a paranormal researcher in New York City before the market tanked. The bottom line is: Otho does whatever he needs to do in order to survive and support his lifestyle. Cheers to you, Otho, and your freelance wheeling and dealing.

SERVINGS 1 • **PREP TIME** 3 MINUTES

INGREDIENTS

- 2 large round ice cubes
- 4 oz black vodka
- 4 oz maraschino cherry juice

GARNISH

- 1 maraschino cherry

DIRECTIONS

❶ Place the ice cubes into a rocks glass. Pour the vodka and cherry juice evenly into the glass.

❷ Cut a slit into the bottom of the cherry and place on rim of glass.

Paint It Black

You can add food dye to create black vodka, but buying black vodka is recommended—it's quite tasty!

THE JAR

Shortly after Tim Burton's feature film debut (see The Big Adventure, pg. 6), he also got a nice TV credit under his belt by helming an episode of *Alfred Hitchcock Presents* titled "The Jar." Based on a short story by Ray Bradbury and the original episode of the same name from Hitchcock's 1960s show (*The Alfred Hitchcock Hour*), "The Jar" was adapted for the '80s art scene by Burton and Michael McDowell—who was the original writer for *Beetlejuice*. This particular episode has all the hallmarks of a Tim Burton creation while feeling very *Beetlejuice*-adjacent—the story follows an unlucky and unappreciated artist struggling for inspiration. It also involves a redheaded female companion, a suicide attempt and a truly bizarre art fixture that captivates/enrages its beholder. While this drink hopefully won't enrage, it is sure to captivate.

SERVINGS 4 • **PREP TIME** 5 MINUTES

INGREDIENTS

- 1 cup fresh blueberries
- 6 oz blue Curaçao
- 8 oz vodka
- 4 oz blueberry schnapps
- 16 oz lemonade
- 4 drops blue cocktail glitter
- 4 oz soda water

GARNISH
- ½ cup fresh blueberries

DIRECTIONS

❶ Layer ice and blueberries into 4 (16-oz) mason jars. In a pitcher, mix blue Curaçao, vodka, blueberry schnapps, lemonade, cocktail glitter and soda water.

❷ Pour an even amount into each jar and garnish with additional blueberries.

THE NETHERWORLD BUREAUCRAT

If Lydia Deetz possesses some of the best zingers in *Beetlejuice*, Otho isn't too far behind. Clever, fashionable and surprisingly incisive, Otho is the living mortal who casually mentions that anyone who commits suicide in life becomes an eternal civil servant in the afterlife. As it turns out, Otho's quip is actually truth: from Juno (see Smoked Brisket, pg. 84) to Miss Argentina (see Miss Argentina Flank Steak, pg. 70), anyone who took their own life ends up pushing pencils in the afterlife. Forever. This drink is in honor of those unfortunate individuals.

SERVINGS 1 • **PREP TIME** 5 MINUTES

INGREDIENTS

- 2 oz gin
- 1 oz sweet vermouth
- ½ oz Campari
- 1 splash triple sec

GARNISH

- 1 orange slice, or kumquat if available

DIRECTIONS

❶ Pour the gin, vermouth, Campari and triple sec into a mixing glass with ice. Stir to dilute and combine.

❷ Pour into a lowball glass with ice. Garnish with orange or kumquat slices.

THE PRINCE VALIUM

W hile "I myself am strange and unusual" is likely Lydia Deetz's most recognizable quote in *Beetlejuice* (see Strange & Unusual, pg. 126), another solid offering is her sarcastic jab at stepmother Delia, whom she describes as "sleeping with Prince Valium tonight" to Barbara and Adam Maitland. A world-weary big-city artist needs her rest, and Prince Valium is reported to be very effective. This nightcap should also do the trick in a pinch, though.

SERVINGS 1 • **PREP TIME** 5 MINUTES
COOK TIME 4 MINUTES

INGREDIENTS

PEA FLOWER TEA
- ½ cup water
- 3 dried pea flowers

- 1 tsp sugar
- 2 oz vodka
- ½ oz blue Curaçao

DIRECTIONS

1 To make pea flower tea, fill a small saucepan with water and boil. Add the pea flowers and sugar, remove from heat and let cool.
2 Chill martini glass in the freezer.
3 Pour ¼ cup of the cooled tea, vodka and blue Curaçao into a large cocktail shaker filled with ice. Shake for 1 minute then strain into the chilled glass.

THE WARNING

Hosting a séance to prove the Winter River home is in fact haunted, Otho reads some chilling lines from *The Handbook for the Recently Deceased* intended to summon the Maitland couple and force them to come face-to-face with the Deetz family. Some of the lines that Otho reads are actually from "The Warning," a poem by 19th-century writer Thomas Lovell Beddoes—a powerful piece that has near-disastrous consequences for Barb and Adam, who are summoned back into their wedding garb as they begin to rapidly age and decay in front of their audience. This take on an old fashioned packs a punch, so it's best to enjoy it responsibly.

SERVINGS 1 • **PREP TIME** 12 MINUTES

INGREDIENTS

1 oz whiskey
1 oz sweet vermouth
2 dashes aromatic bitters

GARNISH
1 sugar cube
1 orange twist
1 maraschino cherry

DIRECTIONS

❶ Add 1 large ice cube to a rocks glass.
❷ Pour the whiskey, vermouth and bitters into a cocktail shaker with ice; stir for 60 seconds to dilute and combine.
❸ Pour into glass. Using the cocktail smoker according to package directions, smoke the cocktail.
❹ Place a sugar cube into the glass and garnish with an orange twist and cherry.

Safe and Simple Smoking at Home

If you've ever been to a fancy bar, you've likely seen, smelled or sipped a smoked cocktail. There are several innovative ways to smoke a cocktail, including lighting a garnish on fire or smoke-rinsing the glass, but these methods can deter the inexperienced (or those who simply aren't fond of the idea of handling a flaming orange peel in their kitchen). For home bartending, one of the best ways to add some smokiness to your spirited concoctions is using a store-bought cocktail smoker. Most cocktail smokers sit atop the glass, allowing you to add smoke to the cocktail itself as well as its serving glass. Some aspiring mixologists and cocktail connoisseurs prefer this method as it provides a bit more smoke flavor than merely smoking the beverage. Smokers differ from brand to brand of course, but each has a container for the combustible contents and a flue that delivers the smoke to the cocktail. Safe and simple!

WATERY GRAVE

Adam and Barbara Maitland's staycation gets off to a rocky start. Agreeing to swing into town to grab some supplies for Adam's model-building, the young couple cross paths with a stray dog (see pg. 106) that trots out in front of their car. In a desperate attempt to avoid hitting said dog, Barb swerves the Maitland Volvo out of the way—and off of a bridge. This cocktail is an homage to the bridge where it all went down, sending Adam and Barbara to their watery grave.

SERVINGS 1 • **PREP TIME** 5 MINUTES

INGREDIENTS

- 5 mint leaves, more for garnish
- ½ oz white rum
- ¼ oz fresh lime juice
- ½ oz simple syrup
- Club soda

GARNISH

- 1 lime slice
- 1 scoop lemon sherbet

DIRECTIONS

❶ Place 5 mint leaves each into 4 tall serving glasses. Using a wooden muddle, muddle the mint, crushing and breaking it up in each glass.

❷ Add ice to each glass. Pour 2 ounces of rum, 1 ounce lime juice and half an ounce simple syrup into each glass and stir.

❸ Top with club soda. Place a mint sprig, lime slice and scoop of lemon sherbet onto each.

GIN & JUICE!
GIN & JUICE!
GIN & JUICE!

There is power in a name, as the old adage goes, and Beetlejuice is no exception. There is also magic in the number three, as discussed by philosophers since Pythagoras and observed in art, nature and beyond. The source of his freedom and his imprisonment, Beetlejuice's Achilles Heel is his own name. And, by saying his name three times, the Maitlands, Lydia Deetz and anyone else who cares to try can summon or banish the Ghost With the Most. This drink will certainly conjure up some fun if you gather a few friends and (for thematic purposes, of course!) slam down three shots each. (Note: Slamming down three of these in a row is a dangerous game recommended only for experienced bio-exorcists.)

MAKES 12 SHOTS • **PREP TIME** 5 MINUTES

INGREDIENTS
- 6 oz black sambuca
- 16 oz lemonade
- 8 oz gin
- 2 egg whites

DIRECTIONS
❶ Add ½ ounce of black sambuca into 12 shot glasses.
❷ Add the remaining ingredients to a shaker and shake for 30 seconds. Add ice and shake for an additional minute.
❸ Carefully strain lemonade mixture evenly into each glass. Using a spoon, scoop the remaining foam onto the top of each shot.

The Flycatcher, pg. 162.

DESSERTS

146 (T)Art in America

148 Dancing Denture Cookies

150 Panna Cotta Eyeballs

152 Gingham Black & White Cookies

154 Jack Skellington Dipped Oreos

156 Dead Mom's Apple Pie

158 My Life is One Big, Dark Mousse

160 Puffed Rice Treat Sculptures

162 The Flycatcher

164 They're Coming to Get You(r Cupcakes), Barbara

166 You're a Pumpkin (Pie)

168 Shakes, Senora

(T)ART IN AMERICA

As mentioned several times in the movie, Delia Deetz is obsessed with *Art in America*—a magazine focused on the hippest, edgiest artists in the country. Her singular goal is to impress others, and there is no better way to signal that she has achieved her goal than by making it into this publication. Delia's art might not be fully appreciated by her movers, her family or her agent, but one of her few endearing qualities is her determination. Viewers never actually get to see her dessert course in the movie (the appetizer, pg. 36, stole the show), but who's to say an avant-garde chocolate spiderweb-y tart isn't what she would have served?

SERVINGS 8–12 • **PREP TIME** 15 MINUTES
COOK TIME 10 MINUTES (PLUS 2 HOURS COOL TIME)

INGREDIENTS

CRUST
- ¾ cup chocolate graham cracker crumbs
- ¾ cup ground walnuts
- ¼ cup light brown sugar
- ½ cup unsweetened cocoa powder
- 6 Tbsp unsalted butter, melted
- ½ tsp vanilla

FILLING
- 12 oz bittersweet chocolate chips
- 1 cup heavy whipping cream
- ¼ cup unsalted butter, cut into small pieces
- ½ Tbsp instant coffee

SPIDERWEB
- 1 tube white decorative icing

DIRECTIONS

❶ Preheat the oven to 350 degrees F.

❷ In a medium bowl, mix together all crust ingredients. Press the crust into the bottom and sides of a 9½-inch tart pan. Bake for 10 minutes, then remove and let cool.

❸ Place the chocolate chips in a separate medium bowl. In a small pan on medium-low heat, bring the heavy cream and butter to a slight simmer. Pour the mixture into the bowl with the chocolate. Mix in the coffee and stir until the chocolate has melted.

❹ Pour the mixture into the cooled crust. Starting in the middle and working out, pipe the icing in a spiral onto the tart. Repeatedly drag a toothpick from the middle to the edge of the tart, about half an inch from the top, to create the spiderweb.

❺ Refrigerate for at least 2 hours.

DANCING DENTURE
COOKIES

After narrowly escaping their own doom thanks to Lydia's help, Barbara and Adam try to save Lydia from a—let's face it—severely creepy underage marriage to a very old demon. Adam desperately tries to say the bio-exorcist's name three times but is ultimately unsuccessful because Beetlejuice pops Adam's teeth out of his mouth. In a delightfully madcap, macabre scene, Adam's disembodied teeth chatter around the house while Beetlejuice tries to stomp them out in a hilarious semi-dance shuffle. These cookies won't dance around your kitchen, but you might after tasting them.

MAKES 12–15 COOKIES • **PREP TIME** 15 MINUTES • **COOK TIME** 30 MINUTES

INGREDIENTS

COOKIES
- 1 cup all-purpose flour
- ¾ cup cocoa powder
- ½ tsp baking soda
- ¼ tsp salt
- 10 Tbsp unsalted butter, room temperature
- ½ cup lightly packed light brown sugar
- ½ cup granulated sugar
- 1 large egg
- ½ tsp vanilla extract
- ½ cup dark chocolate chips
- 2 cups mini marshmallows

BERRY FROSTING
- 2 cups frozen berry mix
- ½ cup sugar
- 2 Tbsp cornstarch
- 8 oz cream cheese, softened
- ¼ cup butter, room temperature
- ½ tsp vanilla extract

DIRECTIONS

❶ Preheat the oven to 350 degrees F.

❷ In a medium bowl, mix together the flour, cocoa powder, baking soda and salt.

❸ In a mixer bowl with paddle attachment, beat the butter and sugars together until fluffy and pale. Mix in the egg and vanilla extract. With the mixer on low, add the flour mixture a little at a time until just combined. Fold in the chocolate chips. Form dough into a thin disk, wrap with plastic wrap and place in the freezer for 10 minutes.

❹ Roll the dough between 2 pieces of parchment paper to ¼-inch thickness. Cut the cookies with a 3½-inch round cookie cutter. Place the cookies onto parchment-lined baking sheets, 1 inch apart. Bake one sheet at a time and refrigerate the cookie sheet that is not being baked.

❺ Bake the cookies for 10 to 12 minutes or until lightly browned at the edges. Remove and cut each in half lengthwise. Let cool for 5 minutes, then place onto a wire cooling rack to cool completely. Repeat with the remaining cookies.

❻ In a small saucepan, cook the berries on medium-low heat until thawed (add a splash of water if needed), then add in the sugar and stir until melted. In a small bowl, mix the cornstarch with a splash of water. Stir the cornstarch into the pan and continue to cook until thickened. Remove from heat and let cool.

❼ Place the cooled berry mixture into a fine mesh sieve and push the mixture through with a rubber spatula (the mixture will be thick).

❽ Beat the cream cheese and butter together until fluffy and smooth, then beat in the vanilla. Fold in the cooled berry mixture to complete the frosting.

❾ Place a layer of frosting onto one side of each cookie. Place the mini marshmallows around the border of half of the cookies. Top the marshmallow cookies with the remaining cookies (frosting side down).

PANNA COTTA EYEBALLS

Beetlejuice still resonates because of the way it plays with horror and comedy genre conventions. A reverse haunted house story in which the unfortunate dead are forced to cohabitate with the intolerable living, the audience sides with the ghosts in the house rather than the intrusive interlopers. After allowing themselves to be photographed and causing a possession scene that only attracts delight and more attention from their unwanted guests, Barbara and Adam are told they must get the Deetz family out of their home by their afterlife caseworker, Juno. Before sending them off this time, though, Juno tells the Maitlands to put on their scary faces and prove they're truly ready for the task—so Barbara and Adam elongate their faces, pop out their eyeballs and give it their all.

MAKES 36–48 EYEBALLS (DEPENDING ON MOLD SIZE) • **PREP TIME** 20 MINUTES
COOK TIME 10 MINUTES (PLUS 5 HOURS COOL TIME)

INGREDIENTS
- 1 (6-oz) package lime Jell-O
- 5 drops red food coloring
- 1 cup milk
- 4 tsp plain gelatin
- 2 cups heavy cream
- ⅓ cup granulated sugar
- 1 tsp vanilla extract
- Non-stick cooking spray
- 1 pint fresh raspberries

DIRECTIONS
❶ Make the Jell-O according to package directions. Take three-quarters of the mixture and place in a container. Mix the red food coloring into the remaining Jell-O to turn it black and place in a separate container. Let both containers cool and set in the refrigerator for about 1 hour.

❷ In a medium saucepan, add the milk and gelatin and whisk to combine. Let sit for 5 minutes. On medium-low heat, bring the mixture to a slight simmer, whisking frequently. Stir in the heavy cream and sugar, whisking until smooth. Remove from the heat and whisk in the vanilla.

❸ Once the Jell-O is set, cut the green Jell-O into half-inch circles for irises (the large end of a piping tip works well). Set aside. Cut the black Jell-O into very small rounds for pupils (use the small end of the piping tip).

❹ Spray round, eye-size molds with non-stick spray. Place a small black pupil in the middle of the green iris rounds, then place the rounds pupil-side down into each mold. Place a raspberry into each. Set the molds on a baking sheet. Pour the panna cotta mixture into the molds and refrigerate for 4 hours or until set.

GINGHAM BLACK & WHITE COOKIES

E very Tim Burton creation has a stylistic point of view. Bold colors, patterns and elongated and bizarre angles all play an important part in his many creative works. It's an interesting contrast when looking at the protagonists of his second feature film: Barbara favors a long prairie gown, whereas Adam rocks a black and white gingham shirt (at one point in their first meeting, Beetlejuice even dons a matching shirt to show how he and Adam are on the same level). Unfortunately for the Maitlands, they died wearing their not-quite-couture garb, meaning they must wear these clothes for, well, eternity. This take on a black and white cookie is an ode to Adam's signature (and forevermore) style.

MAKES 15–18 COOKIES
PREP TIME 20 MINUTES (PLUS 1 HOUR COOL TIME)
COOK TIME 14 MINUTES

INGREDIENTS

- 1   cup butter, softened
- ½   cup granulated sugar
- ¼   tsp vanilla extract
- 2   cups all-purpose flour
-     Pinch salt
- ½   cup unsweetened cocoa
-     Shirt-shaped cookie cutter, optional

DIRECTIONS

❶ Using an electric mixer on high, beat the butter and sugar in a large bowl until fluffy, scraping down the sides as needed. Stir in the vanilla, flour and salt and mix until just combined. Take half the dough out, add in the cocoa and mix until just combined. Wrap the chocolate and plain dough separately in plastic wrap and refrigerate for 1 hour.

❷ On a work surface, roll out each piece of dough to ¼ inch thick. Cut the dough into ½-inch strips. Arrange five strips together, alternating white and chocolate dough. Place five more alternating strips on top. Continue until you have a 9-inch square. Press so the dough stays together. Wrap in plastic wrap and refrigerate for 15 minutes.

❸ Preheat the oven to 350 degrees F.

❹ Take dough out of the refrigerator, slice into ½-inch-thick cookies and place on a parchment-lined cookie sheet. Cut each cookie with the shirt cookie cutter if desired. Bake for 10 to 14 minutes or until the edges are a light golden brown. Remove and let cool for 5 minutes, then transfer onto a wire cooling rack to cool completely.

JACK SKELLINGTON
DIPPED OREOS

Tim Burton has a number of well-known and well-loved films—even the ones geared toward children are stamped with his signature, delightfully ghoulish style. In 1993's *The Nightmare Before Christmas*, a skeleton aptly named Jack Skellington—King of Halloween Town—stumbles into Christmas Town and becomes obsessed. Burton had apparently been drawing Jack Skellington for years before making *The Nightmare Before Christmas*—which is evident in 1988's *Beetlejuice*. When Lydia summons him to save the Maitlands from the botched séance, Beetlejuice literally rises to the occasion—with a Jack Skellington figure perched atop his head.

MAKES 20 COOKIES • **PREP TIME** 10 MINUTES • **COOK TIME** 5 MINUTES

INGREDIENTS

- 24 oz white chocolate chips
- Small skull chocolate molds
- 20 lollipop sticks
- 20 Oreos
- 20 small bat cupcake decorations
- 1 black edible ink pen

DIRECTIONS

❶ Melt the chocolate in a double boiler. Pour into the molds and allow to harden. Remove and set aside. Make 20 skulls.

❷ Place a lollipop stick into each cookie. Dip the cookie into the chocolate, shake off the excess and place on a parchment paper-lined work surface. Place a chocolate skull on the side and a bat on the top. Let cool.

❸ Blacken the eyes, nose and mouth with the pen.

DEAD MOM'S APPLE PIE

One early and defining departure between the film version and the musical version of *Beetlejuice* is the insertion of Lydia's mom. In the movie, we know Charles has an ex-wife who is never named or mentioned on screen (though we do know Delia is not Lydia's biological mom). In the musical, the wife is dead and given a name—Emily—though apparently Charles doesn't like to use her name any more than he acknowledges her in the film. Lydia's deceased mother is actually a root cause of her depression, resentment and anger, as evidenced through the song "Dead Mom." We don't really know what Emily Deetz's signature dessert would be, but Apple Pie is a safe bet.

SERVINGS 8 • **PREP TIME** 20 MINUTES • **COOK TIME** 1 HOUR

INGREDIENTS

CRUST
- 2½ cups unbleached all-purpose flour
- 2 Tbsp sugar
- ¼ tsp salt
- 2 sticks unsalted butter, cut into Tbsp-size pieces
- 6 Tbsp water, very cold
- 1 egg
- 2 Tbsp turbinado sugar

FILLING
- 6 cups sliced apples, Golden Delicious or Honeycrisp
- ½ cup sugar
- ⅓ cup packed brown sugar
- 2 Tbsp all-purpose flour
- ½ tsp cinnamon
- ¼ tsp freshly ground nutmeg
- ¼ tsp salt
- 2 Tbsp unsalted butter

DIRECTIONS

❶ In a food processor, add flour, sugar, salt and butter. Pulse, adding the water into the top feeder until the butter is pea-size. Dump the dough onto a sheet of plastic wrap and push the dough together with your hands, forming 2 disks. Wrap each piece with plastic wrap and refrigerate.

❷ Preheat the oven to 375 degrees F.

❸ In a large bowl, mix together the apples, sugars, flour, cinnamon, nutmeg and salt.

❹ Roll out one disk of dough about 1 inch larger than the pie dish. Place into the pie dish. Place the filling into the pie dish and dollop the top with the butter. Roll the last disk of dough an inch bigger than the pie dish. Place on top and crimp the edges for decoration. Cut an X into the middle to vent.

❺ In a small bowl, whisk the egg and a splash of water together. Brush the crust with the egg wash and sprinkle evenly with the turbinado sugar.

❻ Place the pie onto the lower rack of the oven and bake for 50 to 60 minutes. Cover with foil if the crust starts to get too brown.

❼ Remove and let cool on a wire cooling rack.

MY LIFE IS ONE BIG, DARK MOUSSE

Movie Lydia Deetz may not have the same backstory for her goth rebellion as her Broadway counterpart (see Dead Mom's Apple Pie, pg. 156), but she still carries a fairly large chip on her shoulder. We don't know much about the original Mrs. Deetz, but we do know she's no longer in the picture, which certainly causes some angst for Lydia and tension between her and her stepmom, Delia. Getting uprooted from New York and transplanted to a small town in Connecticut causes even more of that angst—though Charles is quick to strategize by giving Delia full run of the house (with the exception of his office). For Lydia, Charles promises to install a darkroom so she can continue to pursue her photography habit—to which Lydia responds with her classic chutzpah. With this bitter chocolate mousse, you can channel maximum Lydia energy.

SERVINGS 10 • **PREP TIME** 14 MINUTES • **COOK TIME** 10 MINUTES (PLUS 2 HOURS COOL TIME)

INGREDIENTS

- 10 oz semisweet dark chocolate chips
- 8 eggs, separated
- 3 Tbsp water
- 2 cups heavy cream
- 6 Tbsp granulated sugar, divided
- 1 dark chocolate bar, grated, for garnish
- 20 blackberries, for garnish
- 10 sprigs mint, for garnish

DIRECTIONS

❶ Melt the chocolate in a double boiler.

❷ Place the egg yolks and 3 Tbsp of water in a heavy saucepan; cook over very low heat, whisking vigorously and constantly until yolks begin to thicken (about 3 minutes). Remove from heat and pour through a fine mesh sieve.

❸ In a large bowl, fold the melted chocolate into the egg yolk mixture and set aside.

❹ Beat cream with an electric mixer on high until stiff peaks form (about 3 minutes), then slowly beat in 2 Tbsp of sugar. Fold into chocolate mixture.

❺ In a mixer with the whisk attachment, beat egg whites on high speed until soft peaks start to form, about 1 minute. Slowly beat in remaining sugar until stiff peaks form, about 2 to 3 minutes. Fold into chocolate mixture.

❻ Spoon the mousse into 10 serving bowls or cups and place in the refrigerator to cool for 2 hours before serving. Garnish each with grated chocolate, 2 blackberries and a sprig of mint.

PUFFED RICE TREAT SCULPTURES

No one gets between Delia and her art, as she famously threatens Charles when he tells her to take it easy with her remodeling plans. With her avant-garde styling and distinct perspective, Delia is a force to be reckoned with—especially when it comes to remodeling. Her real artistic passion, though, is creating nightmarish, abstract sculptures. This recipe takes a page out of Delia's playbook and invites you to play with your own sculpted treats—after all, anything can be art in the eye of the beholder.

MAKES 9 SCULPTURES • **PREP TIME** 10 MINUTES • **COOK TIME** 5 MINUTES

INGREDIENTS

- 5 Tbsp unsalted butter
- 1 (10-oz) bag mini marshmallows
- 1 cup chocolate chips
- 4 Tbsp cocoa powder
- 5 cups puffed rice cereal
- 9 black Twizzlers

DIRECTIONS

❶ In a large pan, melt the butter and marshmallows on low heat. Add in the chocolate and cocoa and mix to combine. Stir in the puffed rice cereal. Remove from heat.

❷ Quickly form half of the mixture into 2-inch-square blocks and the other half into 2-inch egg shapes. Connect the blocks to the egg shapes with a Twizzler by pushing the licorice into the treats. Set aside to cool.

THE FLYCATCHER

Adam Maitland's scale model of Winter River is as much a character and setting in the film as its life-size namesake. It's the reason Adam and Barbara actually leave their home to go into town, ultimately leading to the couple's watery demise. It's also where Beetlejuice decides to camp out while waiting to take advantage of the freshly deceased Maitlands. While biding his time in the town's cemetery (see Graveyard Dirt Pudding Cups, pg. 96), a hungry Beetlejuice pops his hand out of the ground and urges a fly to come a little closer. Using a Zagnut bar as bait, BJ snatches the fly and drags it underground for a quick nosh. This homemade granola snack offers the same crunchy protein boost, no insect ingredients necessary.

MAKES 14 BARS • **PREP TIME** 5 MINUTES
COOK TIME 20 SECONDS (PLUS 20 MINUTES COOL TIME)

INGREDIENTS

- 1 cup shredded unsweetened coconut
- 1 cup rolled oats
- ½ cup chopped salted peanuts
- 1 cup chopped almonds
- ⅓ cup natural peanut butter
- ¼ cup honey

DIRECTIONS

❶ Line a 9-by-13-inch pan with parchment paper.
❷ In a bowl, mix the coconut, oats, peanuts and almonds. Heat the peanut butter and honey in the microwave for about 20 seconds. Stir this mixture into the coconut mixture. Push the mixture into the pan.
❸ Cover with plastic wrap and refrigerate 20 minutes or until chilled and set.
❹ Cut into 14 even bars.

THEY'RE COMING TO GET YOU(R CUPCAKES), BARBARA

When it comes to groundbreaking works of horror cinema, George A. Romero tends to rank very highly on most lists, most famously for his classic debut feature film, *Night of the Living Dead* (1968). With this film, Romero gave rise to the modern incarnation of the zombie in cinema—often with Johnny's refrain from the opening scene of the film quoted: "They're coming to get you, Barbra." In Tim Burton's *Beetlejuice*, Adam and Barbara Maitland (who adds another "a" to her name) are rumored to have been inspired by Romero's *Night of the Living Dead*, with Lydia even mentioning the film when she first comes face-to-face with the undead couple. In another potential Easter egg, Charles Deetz is seen reading a copy of *The Living and the Dead* magazine at the end of the film. These brain cupcakes are inspired by Barbara's namesake and Romero's classic—just make sure you're ready to defend them with your life, because they're guaranteed to draw a horde.

MAKES 18–20 CUPCAKES • **PREP TIME** 20 MINUTES • **COOK TIME** 35 MINUTES

INGREDIENTS

- ½ cup unsalted butter, room temperature
- 1½ cups sugar
- 2 large eggs, room temperature
- 2½ cups flour
- 3 Tbsp dark cocoa powder
- 1 tsp baking soda
- 1 tsp baking powder
- ¼ tsp salt
- ¾ cup buttermilk
- 1 tsp red food coloring
- 1 tsp vanilla extract
- ½ tsp white vinegar
- 1 cup seedless strawberry jam
- 16 oz cream cheese frosting

DIRECTIONS

❶ Preheat the oven to 350 degrees F.

❷ Line cupcake tins with cupcake liners.

❸ Using an electric mixer with paddle attachment on medium speed, beat the butter and sugar until light and fluffy. Add the eggs one at a time, beating each until fully incorporated. Scrape down the sides of the bowl as needed.

❹ In a large bowl, mix together the flour, cocoa powder, baking soda, baking powder and salt. In a separate medium bowl, whisk together the buttermilk, food coloring, vanilla and vinegar. Add a little of the dry mixture, then wet mixture, continuing to alternate wet and dry, ending with dry mixture. Mix until just combined; do not overmix.

❺ Fill the cupcake liners three-quarters full and bake 25 to 30 minutes or until an inserted toothpick comes out clean. Let cool for 10 minutes. Transfer to a wire cooling rack to cool completely.

❻ In a small saucepan, melt the jam on medium-low heat and strain through a fine mesh sieve. Let cool.

❼ Place the frosting in a piping bag with a medium round tip. Pipe 2 squiggly lines side by side on the cupcake tops, then pipe 2 parallel lines down the middle. Refrigerate to harden the frosting.

❽ Remove from the refrigerator and brush the tops with the cooled jam.

YOU'RE A PUMPKIN (PIE)

As many people can tell you, pet names signal fondness just as often as they can translate to condescension (and at times, both sentiments can be conveyed at once). Michael McDowell and Warren Skaaren's screenplay capitalizes on this dichotomy by using "pumpkin" repeatedly toward both Barbara and Lydia. Jane Butterfield (she of the Buttered Buns, pg. 26), in truly casual cruelty, tells Barbara the house is too big for a couple without children before quickly backtracking by calling Barbara "pumpkin" and assuring her she didn't mean anything by it. Later, when Lydia is trying to tell her father there are ghosts in the house, Charles uses "pumpkin" to shoo her away. This pie might not be able to stop folks from being condescending jerks, but it will get them to do less talking and more eating.

SERVINGS 4–6 • **PREP TIME** 10 MINUTES • **COOK TIME** 50 MINUTES

INGREDIENTS

CRUST
- 1 cup graham cracker crumbs
- ½ cup crushed pecans
- ¼ cup sugar
- 5 Tbsp butter, melted

FILLING
- 3 eggs
- ¼ cup brown sugar
- 1¼ cups ricotta cheese
- 2 cups pumpkin puree
- ¼ tsp salt
- 1 tsp pumpkin pie spice
- ½ tsp cinnamon
- 1 tsp vanilla extract

DIRECTIONS
❶ Preheat the oven to 350 degrees F.
❷ In a medium bowl, mix all crust ingredients. Grease a 9½-inch tart pan with butter, add crust mixture and press into the bottom and sides.
❸ Using a mixer with a paddle attachment, mix eggs and sugar until well blended. Add remaining ingredients and mix until just combined. Pour pumpkin mixture into the crust and bake for 50 minutes or until an inserted toothpick comes out clean. Cool to room temperature and refrigerate.

SHAKES, SENORA

Another iconic scene in *Beetlejuice* takes place at the end of the movie, with the Deetzes and the Maitlands now (un)living in harmony after vanquishing Beetlejuice. Lydia, who appears to be making friends at school, races home and informs the Maitlands that she got an A on her math test—and therefore gets treated to a floating, football player ghost rendition of Harry Belafonte's "Jump in the Line (Shake, Senora)." This milkshake, inspired by the "Shake, shake, shake Senora" lyric, also doubles as a sweet reward for a job well done.

SERVINGS 4 • **PREP TIME** 5 MINUTES

INGREDIENTS

- 1 (16-oz) tub chocolate Icing
- 6 oz mini marshmallows
- 32 oz chocolate milk
- 8 scoops chocolate brownie ice cream
- 1 (6½-oz) can whipped cream
- ⅓ cup chocolate sprinkles

DIRECTIONS

❶ Spread a generous amount of the chocolate icing on the top inch of the outer rim of 4 large serving glasses. Press the mini marshmallows into the icing.
❷ Fill each glass with 8 oz of chocolate milk and add 2 scoops of ice cream. Top each evenly with whipped cream and sprinkles.

INDEX

A

Ahi tuna, 38
Ale, pale, 20
Almond(s), 163
   extract, 94
   milk, 15
Apple(s), 119, 122, 156
   cider, 122
Avocados, 16, 25, 38, 40, 65

B

Bacon, 6, 12, 69, 76, 116
Baking powder, 6, 62, 93, 109, 164
Baking soda, 6, 20, 93, 149, 164
Balsamic glaze, 9
Bananas, 15, 93
Bat cupcake decorations, 155
Beans, cannellini, 22
Beef
   brisket, 84
   flank steak, 70

   ground, 66, 76, 88
   sirloin steak, 55
   skirt steak, 64
Beer, Mexican, 62
Berry mix, frozen, 149
Bitters, aromatic, 137
Blackberries, 15, 105, 119, 159
Blueberries, 15, 133
Bread
   brioche buns, 76
   crumbs, 66, 69, 88
   panko, 69
   French baguette, 30
   sprouted grain, 16
   white, 88
Broccoli, frozen, 59
Broth
   beef, 30
   chicken, 44, 48, 51, 52, 59
Brown sugar, 20, 47, 52, 83, 84, 87, 93,
   101, 146, 149, 156, 167

Buttermilk, 164

C

Cabbage, green, 52
Cake mix, strawberry, 73
Campari, 134
Candy eyes, 102, 105
Capers, 60
Caramel, 33
Carrots, 48, 51, 52, 72
Cashews, 15
Caviar, black roe, 38
Celery, 48, 51, 52, 72, 116
Cereal
   puffed rice, 160
   wheat, 6
Champagne, 119
Cheese
   American, 76
   blue, 28
   Brie, 105

cheddar, 9, 20, 65, 69, 106
  habanero, 20
cotija, 34
cream, 60, 149
Gruyère, 12, 30, 69
mozzarella, 60
Parmesan, 60, 106
Pecorino Romano, 88
pepper jack, 105
queso blanco, 62
ricotta, 167
Cherries, maraschino, 115, 130, 137
Cherry spreadable fruit, 79
Chicken, 56, 64, 87
  breasts, 52, 59, 75, 80
  with wing bone attached, 60
  thighs, 51
  wing drumettes, 28
Chocolate
  chips, 146, 149, 155, 159, 160
  dark, 105, 109, 159
  melts, 33
  milk, 168
  pudding, 97
  sprinkles, 168
  white, 102
Coarse salt, 20
Cocktail glitter, 133
Cocoa powder, unsweetened, 109, 146, 149, 152, 160, 164
Coconut, 25
  shaved, unsweetened, 10, 125, 163
  sugar, 10
Coffee, instant, 146
Cole slaw mix, 62
Cookies, strawberry shortcake, 73
Corn, 34, 73
Corn syrup,
Cornstarch, 52, 75, 149
Crab leg clusters, 116

Crackers, 105
  graham, 146, 167
Crema, 65
Cucumber, 28
Curaçao, 112, 133, 137

D
Dates, 10

F
Flowers, dried pea, 137
Food coloring, 98, 150, 164
Frosting, cream cheese, 164

G
Garlic, 26, 28, 34, 40, 47, 51, 55, 56, 59, 60, 64, 65, 66, 70, 75, 79, 80, 83, 88, 106
  black, 37
Gelatin, 150
Gin, 129, 134, 142
Ginger, 47, 75, 120
Ginger ale, 119
Ginger beer, 126
Grapes, 105
Grenadine, 115
Gummies, 112

H
Halibut fillets, 62
Ham, 47
Heavy cream, 44, 59, 146, 150, 159, 168
Herbs
  basil, 26, 40, 88
  chives, 9, 12, 22, 40
  cilantro, 25, 62, 65, 80
  dill, 40
  mint, 73, 79, 141, 159
  parsley, 22, 26, 40, 51, 55, 60, 88
  rosemary, 26, 48
  sage, 44, 48

  thyme, 26, 48, 120
Honey, 10, 62, 83, 163
Horseradish, cream-style, 73

I
Ice cream, chocolate brownie, 168
Icing
  white, 146
  chocolate, 168

J
Jell-O, lime, 150
Juice
  beet, 120
  cranberry, 115
  lemon, 16, 22, 28, 37, 40, 56, 60, 120
  lime, 25, 34, 62, 64, 65, 115, 116, 141
  maraschino cherry, 130
  orange, 75
  pineapple, 47, 115
  tomato, 116

K
Ketchup, 47, 83, 87
Kiwi, 15
Kosher salt, 55
Kumquat, 134

L
Lamb, racks, 79
Lemonade, 133, 142
Lemon(s), 22, 56
  juice, see Juice
  sherbet, 141
Lettuce, 65
  bib, 64
  dark leaf, 76
Limes, 62, 80, 116, 125, 141
  juice, see Juice
Lobster, 69

M

Marshmallows, 149, 160, 168
Mayonnaise, 28, 34, 37, 40, 62, 72, 73, 76
Microgreens, 16
Mushrooms, portobello, 64
Mustard, 83
    Dijon, 20, 37, 40, 72, 79, 87
    yellow, 73

N

Nori sheets, 38
Nuts
    almonds, *see Almonds*
    peanuts, 163
    pecans, 101, 167
    pistachios, 10
    walnuts, 146

O

Oats, 163
Olive(s)
    black, 105, 116
    brine, 129
    green, 40, 105, 129
Onions, 48, 51, 66
    green, 52, 72, 75
    red, 25, 47, 62, 65
    yellow, 30, 59, 80, 88
Orange(s), 119, 120, 122, 134
    marmalade, 75
    twist, 137
Oreos, 97, 155

P

Pasta
    cellentani, 59
    chow mein broad noodles, 52
    egg noodles, 51
    elbow macaroni, 72
    orzo, 60

    spaghetti, 88
    tortellini, cheese, 69
Peanut butter, 15, 163
Peppermint extract, 109
Pepperoni, 105
Peppers
    Carolina reaper, 28
    chilaca, 80
    green bell, 66, 80
    jalapeño, 25, 28, 65
    mini red, 12, 70, 80
    orange, 59
    red bell, 47, 66, 72
    roasted red, 22, 55
    serrano, 70
    yellow, 80
Pineapple, 47, 115
Pizza dough, 106
Popcorn kernels, 33
Pork
    chops, 44
    ribs, 87
    sausages, breakfast, 6
Powdered sugar, 93
Pretzels, 20, 102
    mini twist, 105
Prosciutto, 105
Pumpkin puree, 167
Punch, Berry Blue Typhon
    Hawaiian, 112

R

Raspberries, 150
    jam, 105
Rice, black, 38
Rum, 112
    banana, 115
    black spiced, 126
    Jamaican, 93
    pineapple, 115
    white, 141

Rumchata, 125, 126

S

Salami, 105
Salmon fillets, 83
Sambuca, black, 142
Sauce
    barbecue, 73
    horseradish, 116
    hot, 9, 20, 25, 28, 62, 83, 87, 116
    marinara, 66, 88
    soy, 38, 47, 52, 64, 75, 83
    steak, 87
    Worcestershire, 20, 66, 116
Schnapps, blueberry, 133
Sea salt, 33
Seasoning
    avocado toast, 17
    blackened, 37
    everything bagel, 16
    fajita, 80
Seeds
    flax, 10
    pumpkin, 10
    sesame, 10, 20, 38, 75, 83
Sesame oil, 52
Shallots, 60
Sherry, 30
Shrimp, 37
Soda
    lemon-lime, 112
    water (club), 133, 141
Sour cream, 28, 34, 38, 65
Spices
    anise pods, 122
    basil, 60
    Cajun seasoning, 59, 72
    cayenne pepper, 28, 64, 73, 84, 101
    celery seeds, 62, 116
    chili powder, 64, 84

cinnamon, 93, 101, 156, 167
  stick, 119, 122
cloves, whole, 122
cream of tartar, 98
cumin, 25, 34, 64, 65, 84
garlic powder, 64, 84, 87
herbes de Provence, 30
mustard powder, 84
nutmeg, 69, 122, 156
Old Bay seasoning, 116
onion powder, 56, 60, 70, 84, 87
oregano, 55, 56, 64, 70
paprika, 20, 34, 56, 60, 70, 116
  smoked, 64, 84, 87
parsley, 60, 66, 70, 72, 84, 106
pumpkin pie, 167
red pepper flakes, 28, 55, 70,
  75, 79
rosemary, 55
thyme, 84
Spinach, fresh, 60
Stock, *see Broth*
Strawberries, 6, 73, 119
  jam, 164

Sweet potatoes, 16
Syrup, 141

T
Taco shells, 64
Tequila, 112, 116, 120, 125
Tomatoes, 9, 25, 65, 70
  cherry, 59
  grape, 59
  yellow, 76
Tortillas
  corn, 62, 64
  flour, 80
Triple sec, 125, 134
Turbinado sugar, 156
Turkey, 48
Twizzlers, 160

V
Vanilla extract, 6, 15, 94, 98, 101,
  109, 146, 149, 150, 152,
  164, 167

Vermouth
  dry, 129
  sweet, 134, 138
Vinegar
  apple cider, 22, 65, 73, 87
  balsamic, 55
  distilled, 65
  red wine, 55, 70
  white, 164
Vodka, 112, 133, 137
  black, 130

W
Whipped topping, 73, 97
Whiskey, 138
Wine
  red, 119
  white, 30, 60

Y
Yeast, 20, 25
Yogurt, 56
  Greek, 15, 40

ACKNOWLEDGMENTS

I LIKE TO think of nostalgia- and genre-inspired cookbooks as works of culinary fan fiction—this cookbook is the biggest fanfic trip down memory lane I've ever had the pleasure of taking. None of it would have been possible without the incredibly creative and supportive team at Media Lab Books. A huge thank you to Phil Sexton for the idea behind the project, Jeff Ashworth for the helpful feedback and idea-tweaking, Juliana Sharaf for her exceptional editing and the biggest of shout-outs to Trevor Courneen for wrangling everything and keeping us all on task!

This book could not have happened without the wildly talented Isabel Minunni, the best partner-in-culinary-crime a gal could ever want. Your inspired recipes, big flavors and enthusiasm are a joy, and I'm so glad we have another cookbook under our collective belts.

To Ben Kolansky, my life-partner-in-crime, thank you for putting up with me and my weird ideas, for listening to me spout off *Beetlejuice* trivia and for enduring multiple re-watches (complete with pauses and rewinds) in the name of research.

A huge thank you to the source material: I have watched *Beetlejuice* 167-ish times and it keeps getting funnier every single time I see it! It's an important film to me, and I'm thrilled to be able to celebrate it with fans. Which brings me to you, fellow nerd. Thank you for reading this book. I hope it inspires you to turn on the juice and see what shakes loose.

—THEA JAMES

I WOULD LIKE to express the deepest appreciation to Media Lab Books for all their hard work on the collaboration of this book.

Thank you to Phil Sexton for trusting me to be part of your amazing team. I am grateful for Trevor, Juliana and Jeff for all their editing skills. I often mention to my family and friends how much I appreciate their hard work! Also a big thanks to Courtney for overseeing the project and to the entire team for their special talents that make my recipes shine! And Tom Mifsud, thank you for the introduction to this great team!

Thea James, it has been my absolute pleasure to work with you again on this project. You are an amazingly talented writer and I am proud to collaborate with you.

Thank you to my husband for being my constant support, believing in me, being my honest taste tester and making sure I always had a well-stocked pickle supply (oddly my favorite snack while writing). Thank you to my children for poking their heads into my office to say hi and to see if I needed anything, like a pickle or a beverage. Telling me you are proud of me is the best thing a mother can hear!

—ISABEL MINUNNI

ABOUT THE AUTHORS

THEA JAMES is the coauthor of *Cooking for Wizards, Warriors and Dragons* and *Drinking with Wizards, Warriors and Dragons*. She is also the cofounder and editor of *The Book Smugglers*, a Hugo Award-winning science fiction and fantasy book review blog. A hapa (half) Filipina-American who was born in Hawaii and grew up in Indonesia and Japan before moving to the United States, Thea is a passionate advocate for the importance of diverse voices in SFF. She is a full-time book nerd who works in publishing and currently resides in Marlboro, New York, with her partner and rambunctious cat.

ISABEL MINUNNI is a cook, recipe developer, food writer and the coauthor of cookbooks including *The 28-Day Pegan Diet* and *Cooking for Wizards, Warriors and Dragons*. She created the popular food blog Bella's Banquet (*bellasbanquet.com*) and has won numerous food and baking competitions, including being named 2014's "Best Italian Chef" by Chef Jeff Mann and Maggiano's Little Italy restaurant chain. One of her favorite cookie recipes was selected from among 4,000 entries for inclusion in *The Barnes & Noble Cookie Bake-Off*. Her numerous TV appearances include both *Today* and *Live! With Kelly and Michael*.

Media Lab Books
For inquiries, call 646-449-8614

Copyright © 2023 by Media Lab Books

Published by Topix Media Lab
14 Wall Street, Suite 3C
New York, NY 10005

Printed in China

ISBN-13: 978-1-956403-29-9
ISBN-10: 1-956403-29-9